CROSSING
THE BARRIER
to the light of
EXPANDED CONSCIOUSNESS

NESSA ALGIE

Mind body spirit healing insight. Whilst transpersonal psychology aptly addresses the 'art of self awareness'. Karmic psychology dares to go that one step further. To incorporate reincarnation and all its implications... All encompasing evolutionary consciousness.

Nessa reveals throughout the text that by transcending the myths of religion and mysticism and going beyond ritual, dispelling, letting go of some new age beliefs *will initiate healing,* at the cellular level.

The secret is to use knowledge not just to simply accumulate it! We must learn to communicate openly and honestly, with integrity and heart. Sometimes divine wisdom does shock, especially when one is not quite prepared for it! It is choice now that determines whether we apply this knowledge or not! 'What you sow so shall you reap.' Nessa states categorically.

The chapters on sexuality, love, neutrality and liberation are certainly food for thought. The seeds of change will have been sown, if not this lifetime, then another! Healing and self empowerment is an art, after all. It moves us from the space of self-centredness to self-awareness - from helplessness to wholeness.

One of the greatest misconceptions is the mystery of Kundalini. In the past it was only understood by those who studied and embraced eastern culture. Through Nessa's initiation it has at last been unveiled for the benefit of western society in order to finally unite eastern and western philosophies.

Great philosophers, seers, sages and disciples obviously faced overwhelming obstacles. It must have taken supreme courage and supreme power to 'over come to become.'

To change opinion, it is necessary to swim against the flow of tide.

Reality based spirituality, ethical practice, honourable intent and down to earth practicality are needed now more than ever.

In order to make the transition smoothly into the 21st. Century and beyond we need to lighten up, explore universal law and expand our consciousness.

Numerology and astrology have been used in the past to determine life's purpose - they are still valuable sciences today. Nessa's expertise is reflected in this volume, providing yet another tool for divination. When we are told we have chosen our role, our parents, our lessons, it is hard to believe. However to transcend illness it is fundamental that we understand this.

This text will undoubtedly revolutionise modern mans/womans thinking. Humanity will evolve still further and perception of our world, our earth school will be changed forever!

Thank you Nessa

Sarah Steenstra - Bloomfield RN.DIP.N Sc.

Transpersonal/Karmic Psychologist

Complementary Health Practitioner

What then are barriers? *Barriers* are the blockages we perpetually create with the mind - from our perceptions of right and wrong - truth and illusion. Unless we have reached the stage of neutrality we will always create negativity through action and/or reaction. Life does not automatically change through external circumstances. It is only through the ability to change perception do we eventually liberate ourselves from the quagmire of fundamental existence. So what are we really on the earth plane for? To change, to grow, to evolve and to transcend all limitation and bondage from *baser* physical, emotional, mental and spiritual anarchy.

My journey to *expanded consciousness* began in May 1978. This created dramatic and catalytic changes in my life and in the lives of those around me. Prior to this I had been brought up with a Christian faith but by '74, I had started to question the validity of many of the teachings in the Bible and wanted to find the truth. Books based on the Eastern philosophies eventually *found me* and through these I was exposed to other mystical explanations of life, death and rebirth.

In the mean time my *initiation* involved the irrational world - the world I couldn't see - and included heartaches, loss, pain and denial of the greatest magnitude through a *'supreme power'*. I was introduced to Numerology in late 1986 and because I needed to structure 'this higher spiritual awakening' into a more tangible feasibility, it gave me the opportunity for focusing this expansion into greater understanding of esoteric truths.

May I add this is not a Numerology book! (Magnets of the Universe - Numerology into the 21st Century explains the new Karmic numbers I have invented in this ancient science) I have simply used Numerology throughout this book to explain the meaning of words like sin, love, man, woman, spirit, etc. and to also define certain Karmic lessons. To reach an expanded consciousness is not an easy process and for some it may take many lifetimes because of the negative perceptions, actions and reactions we crystallise in our day to day existence.

The time has definitely arrived for massive changes and if this has to come about through eruptions, heartache and pain - it will! This will always depend on our ability to accept change not to resist it. The Karmic and evolutionary wheel keeps turning and we keep turning with it......

There are many books written on life, death and afterlife experiences and these have greatly affected mass consciousness to question our very existence. This book encompasses these subjects also. However it's ultimate purpose is to teach you how to live through truth and light! The here and now! The ability to reach immortality of the *spirit* from the chains which bind us to the perpetual cycle of life, death and rebirth. The lesson is the same for each and every one of us! The only thing which is different is how much we want to change. Everything comes back to personal choice! *This is Karma!* Through initiating new ideas and ideals in our lives we can all begin our own and ultimate journey 'Crossing The Barrier To The Light of Expanded Consciousness'.

Nessa Algie
P.O. Box 359
Cannington 6107
(Perth) Western Australia

CHAPTER   1

"All journeys have a single purpose - to get to another place. There are places everywhere and the differences are less than you might think - Some places, are just a state of mind."

Karma - The conception of the quality of actions including both merit and demerit of inevitable consequence which generate the result of the actions of life. There are many misconceptions about Karma! Karma is the Universal law of justice - the law of cause and effect! *'What we sow we will reap'* - from one lifetime to the next, the next and even the next. Karma is choice! The choice between positive and negative, good and bad. All negative and positive actions from our past and present lives will ultimately create negative or positive conditions for our present or future lifetimes. Karma exists for all individuals eventually - as well as all countries. Karma therefore gives us the ability to try again and again and again - to ultimately evolve to greater heights of wisdom through positive self-empowerment, physically (materially), emotionally, mentally and spiritually.

When we choose our lives for rebirth to the earth plane we all have the opportunity to pick our parents from two or three prospective candidates. Sometimes these choices have Karmic implications either positive or negative from previous lifetimes. Because we pick from the spirit world we know of course what we ultimately have to learn. In

Karma is free will! It is choice! But please do not continually use this excuse for creating negativity in your life. Through the continual use of negative energies we set up patterns and conditioning which require a greater deal of effort to overcome. Karma is also cause and effect! What goes round comes around! We will always reap what we sow from one lifetime to the next - to the next - and even the next. Karma gives us all the ability to choose - the positive versus the negative - the light versus the darkness!

So through trials, obstacles, heartaches and unfulfilment over many, many lifetimes it is hoped we will eventually choose the right path. There are many who negate right for wrong - light for darkness - truth for illusion in their quest for love, power, glory, authority, spirituality, success and acclaim. The path of least resistance and one of negativity is *not* the path we are meant to travel. Many of the lessons we have come back to learn will require strength, discipline, discernment, responsibility and self-empowerment of the greatest magnitude.

Numerologically speaking *sin* vibrates to 15/6 - the Tarot symbolism of the 15/6 - '*The Devil.*' This vibration means limitation and bondage *or* freedom - the choice is yours! To rise above greed, egotism and emotional dependencies. To rise above the baser animal nature! This is the journey of darkness and will always bring a life of limitation and bondage not just to the earth plane but to others and worse still to ourselves.

The prize - *freedom* and living life through a much higher comprehension of *love consciousness*. Through these energies we have the ability to regenerate and to transcend which in turn brings a greater depth of understanding. This transcendence gives us the honour to aspire to higher dimensions. Bondage to people, things and feelings - is bondage to the earth plane.

The word sin begins with S. S is the 19th. Letter of the alphabet. It is the letter of surrender - to the grave and back - or to death and back. Through repeated negative patterning and conditioning this is exactly what happens.

Therefore it becomes imperative we *overcome to become* and transcend all earthly illusions and the continual cycle of life, death and rebirth. In the Tarot the 19 symbolises the Sun. Negatively it scorches and burns those who misuse this power but used positively, it allows light and growth.

All our heartaches, trials, obstacles and challenges in life will eventually help us to penetrate this world of inevitability allowing us to comprehend and understand ourselves and ' *The Meaning of Life.'* This is *self-awareness!* Once this state has been accomplished one is well on the way and the next steps become easier. The higher one evolves the more insight and wisdom one achieves.

> **"Each life has its way, each way is a journey and to leap to its end, is like jumping from birth to death."**

Civilisations come and go and now we are on the threshold of a new age, The Age of Aquarius (key phrase - I Know) the *Age Of Truth And Knowledge* It is time to let go of the rigid ideas, deception and the delusions of our last age -The Age Of Pisces. However what we can hang onto from this age is love and faith. These qualities we must expand upon to encompass a greater dimension of reality to take forward with us into the new age. It is time to open and expand our vision. To let go of the dogma, superstitions, rituals and fantasies of the past.

When it is time to enter The Age Of Capricorn (key phrase - I Use) approximately 2000 years from now, humanity will take Truth, Knowledge and Humanitarian Love from the Age Of Aquarius. They will *use* these traits with those of the Age Of Capricorn - discrimination, responsibility, strength and discipline for self empowerment to climb to the top of the mountain on all planes of existence. The ultimate achievement of course is *wisdom*! Truth, Knowledge and Love are useless without the ability to *use* them for all Karmic and evolutionary growth and development.

What then is attainment - without truth, knowledge and universal love? (The traits of our Aquarian Age) It would not be Wisdom! Each and every age is essential for the evolution of humankind. Of course as individuals we do not have to wait for The Age Of Capricorn to achieve these pinnacles of wisdom. This is free will - this is choice! This is a journey we can all begin right now!

"Today is the first day of the rest of your life."

There are many, many, new changes ahead for humanity. To create change, old traditions, philosophies, belief systems, structures, ideals and attitudes have to fall. This then makes way for new *truth and knowledge* with universal love to be shared by all. Each and everyone of us is on earth to learn, to evolve, to overcome, to transform, to regenerate and to transcend. We all have the ability to attain our freedom

- our liberation therefore the sooner we become aware the sooner we can achieve.

Spirituality is - the expansion and knowledge of the spirit, our own spirit. The spirit which is within each and every one of us. It is the completeness and power of the inner self through individualisation and the attainment of *God Consciousness.* God Consciousness is the expansion of the spirit to higher realms of understanding through the purity of mind, heart and deed! True spiritually must come from within - from the Karmic and evolutionary growth of our soul.

Spirituality is not - rigid conditioning, it is not fear, guilt, prejudice, tunnel vision, male dominance, (patriarchy) manipulative power, authority, politics, man made laws, ownership, enslavement, the power of the church, secrecy, agony, oppression or ritual.

As an Ancient Philosophy states

"Even Heaven is merely a resting place on the way,
Like every soul we are reborn again and again til
we attain enlightenment.
The journey is endless: The end is to stop travelling.
Do you know that is NOT the same thing,
as staying where you are?
Then travel til you learn that you must get off
the road.
Learn there is no road, journey or pilgrims, only
freedom!"

To be just spiritual is not the key to liberation. There are many grades of spirituality just as there are many grades of evolutionary growth and development. Life is a school and as with school if we do not pass the tests we will come back and repeat them.

Positive action receives positive Karma and positive action is not, "I'll scratch your back if you scratch mine" or "What's in it for me?" This may be the basis for a business agreement and perhaps there is nothing wrong with it but do not think this is *giving*! Positive Karma is earned through helping, doing, caring, giving from the heart unconditionally. It is honouring our commitments - but this does not mean we have to give ourselves in useless self-sacrifice. Useless self-sacrifice creates spite, bitterness, resentment, jealousy and hate. There are of course those rare individuals who have literally given their lives to save someone else. This will create very positive Karma because they come from complete selflessness and love with no thought of payment or regret.

When giving don't expect something in return as Karmic payments don't necessarily come from the person you give to but will be repaid in some other way and at some other time, even some other lifetime. If you do not give with the right motives with a free heart, you may not get back what you want. Karma is not "If I give to you, you will give to me in return". It is, what *goes around - comes around* - not always instantly but it will happen eventually. It is the consequence of all actions and reactions. This is cause and effect.

So what does the word *freedom* conjure up for you? Freedom means not only letting go, acceptance, expansion, faith, giving, optimism and happiness but transcendence, light and love. No room for rigid patterns here!

Freedom and liberation - is the freedom of the spirit from physical reality. Physical reality is really *the illusion*! We must all exonerate past and present conditioning, patterning and negative attitudes. These create the habits which constrict, bind and limit us to a life of servitude to earthly encumbrances. *Hanging on* to earthly manifestations prolongs our upward journey to the light and finding eternal joy and love for all.

The mind - the rational. The spirit - the irrational - but only because it cannot be seen! Yet most of us know we have a spirit. Therefore this poses the question, "What is true reality - and what is illusion?" Do not delude yourself this is not all that there is to our existence! "What then is physical reality?" This is the reality of the physical world and the physical world is really *the illusion* because this is only a transitory world - this is our earth school. The world where we come to reverse our negative patterning - to learn - to change - to grow - to evolve - to attain - to transcend and then to leave.

Therefore we cannot believe in it completely! A world full of seductions and imperfections until we 'overcome to become'. Physical reality of the physical world is a temporary fatuity and is only the kindergarten for greater achievement and attainment. Achievement therefore is essential for all evolutionary and Karmic growth! To grow, to evolve, to attain, to understand, to uplift, to believe in self and others, to care, to empower, to change, to transform, to regenerate, to transcend and to find neutrality. This is wisdom! This is Karma! This is justice! This is freedom!

As we expand our consciousness - and search for our own spirituality we will still experience feelings of unhappiness, unfulfilment and even desolation because our lives require deeper insight into the conceptive substantiality of all existence. Spirituality therefore is all encompassing, it is a growing thing as perpetual as time itself and comes from *conscious growth*. So it stands to reason why we must not forget to feed the very core of our being - our inner light - our very soul - our higher consciousness. That special part of us which seeks immortality - the transcendence of all earthly manifestations.

If we forgot to feed the body we would definitely die, so it stands to reason why we must elevate and nurture that which is within us, our own divine spirit. Many find prayer uplifts and nourishes and many others use meditation. This not only brings purification of the mind, peace, balance, control, but insight and higher expansion. Positive spiritual affirmations and philosophies are also an excellent way to bring progress and change to our conceptual existence. Always create beauty within yourself through inner reality. If you need the company of others, make sure they are on your own spiritual level.

Numerologically speaking *spirit* vibrates to the energies of 37/1. The base number 1 means: Belief in self, action, individualisation, motivation, courage, creation and will. Working through the 7 - Conquest of the mental plane. The power to control the mind! To think rationally but to also go within and find the seeds of life through rest, solitude and meditation. This creates the ability to expand the mind to encompass even higher realms of consciousness - the true reality of our existence - the mystical and spiritual! 7 is inner reality which is what our spirit is! Working through the 3 - the light of life - the light of the spirit - through hope, faith, love, acceptance, creativity, optimism and happiness. This is expansion! This is freedom! There is no room for rigid perceptions here!

Spirit has a soul of 18/9. It is an emotional energy and can be very deceptive if we centre on just ourselves. This vibration creates the ability to bring the body, mind and higher mind together. The only way we can expand our spirituality is through conscious growth. 9 is the humanitarian - It is Universal love! In the Tarot it is symbolised by the *Moon*. The outer personality of the word *spirit* is the 19/1. Individualisation, independence, belief in self, action and force. It is the number of surrender. Paying back Karmic debts - to death and back - to the grave and back. This then explains how the spirit evolves - through reincarnation - to death and back the cycle of life, death and rebirth. The Tarot symbolism *The Sun*.

The light of the moon comes from the sun! This is the same for humanity. The growth of our spirit comes from the evolutionary growth of the *conscious mind*. Our soul like the moon cannot become *light* unless it has the light of the sun or the light of the conscious mind to create.

> ***"Speak words of kindness.***
> ***One who speaks angry words***
> ***is destroyed by the weapon***
> ***of his own speech."***
>
> *"The Way of Kings."*
> *Ancient Wisdom from the Sanskrit Vedas*
> *Translated by Drew Lawrence.*

Judging by the negativity which exists in the world today, we can see why it takes so long to expand spiritual consciousness! We must all understand we can and must reverse the negative patterning, conditioning, habits and attitudes of our past and present lifetimes. There will always be conflict until we transform and transcend these defeating energies. Negative versus positive! - right versus wrong! - light versus darkness! Illusion versus reality! We must all eventually choose the right path - so why not now? Change and grow! Cross the barrier and journey to the light of a higher awareness.

We are all affected by Karma! Individuals, countries and even civilisations. Therefore it is interesting to note approximately 2,600 years ago humanity had reached an important crossroad in evolutionary growth. Much of this culture came from Ionian thinkers. Asian mysticism, mingled with the Greeks need for pragmatic analysis to create an age of philosophers, poets, writers, sculptors, potters, scientists, architects, mathematicians and an age of physical fitness. (The Olympic games were in progress as well).

We are now repeating very similar patterns but thankfully most of us are operating from higher planes of consciousness. The following is documentation on this past age:

"New ideas, ideals, attitudes and beliefs geared to attaining a better life and understanding of life became obvious in many parts of the world. It was as if humanity was being moved by a universal consciousness to aspire to greater things, to lift itself to a higher realm of existence."

This was the Age of Aries. The 'I Am.' The evolutionary and Karmic wheel had turned and humanity started to question personal idenity - 'the who and what they were'.

These were the questions being asked at the time: "What choices about the patterns of existence does humanity have? What are the consequences of choice? What of the human condition in all of it's complexities and frailties? How can humanity understand the implications of a world which contain both good and evil, kindness and cruelty?" These are questions which at last after 2,600 years have answers.

This was the time when there were Goddesses - women who were respected, honoured and revered for their knowledge and wisdom. These Goddesses were created from the legends and myths of the women who were chosen as well as men, in their celestial duty as 'Gardeners of the Earth.' These legends live on! Athena, Aphrodite, Dianne, Isis, Hathor, Maat. This patterning is re-emerging but *only* because all women must empower themselves. The Etruscan civilisation flourished in the 6th Century B.C. This was a civilisation where women were completely equal.

The patterns are similar - but the reality this time? To question our place in the 'higher scheme of things!' To know and understand a much greater realm of truth! Perhaps humanity is questioning who and what they are not through just a universal consciousness as in the past but through a higher dimension of spiritual consciousness - *through truth and love - humanitarian love!* (The traits of the Aquarian Age) The Karmic and evolutionary wheel keeps turning and we must turn with it.

Today a new reality is in existence which is expressed in the following quote: "Higher spiritual energies are changing mass consciousness. Humanity is becoming aware of its inner soul energies. This awakening is changing humankind's approach to the meaning of life. A change of consciousness must be experienced if we are to solve the many intricate problems of this age. The challenge then is to bring love, integrity, morality, divine compassion and humanitarianism to the world."

We are on the threshold of this age, the age of unity for all humankind though love, truth and knowledge. Of all the civilisations humanity has experienced so far, the new age will be the most advanced and spiritual. The age of Aquarius will not provide all the answers as humanity will have to learn to use their abilities before they can achieve wisdom. What this age creates will provide the nucleus for the last age, 'The Age of Capricorn'. This is the ultimate! When *all* humankind will have the ability to use their energies to empower themselves through wisdom. Individually we can all choose to journey on the path which leads to this elevated state whenever we wish. This is choice - this is free will.

"Know that wisdom is such to your soul;
if you find it, there will be a future, and your hope
will not be cut off."

It takes a great deal of time for evolutionary growth to eventuate. Even civilisations repeat patterns. However as it progresses the new knowledge available should create expansion 'into higher truths. Eventually this creates change for individuals and for mass consciousness as well. This is our evolutionary growth - this is our Karmic reward. We must not worship the past or hang onto it through ignorance, superstition or fear although of course we should learn from it. We do not need to go backwards but look to the present and future. The past always makes the present, makes the future.

> *" My journey has started*
> *I feel ready - enthused.*
> *What will the past*
> *Teach me -*
> *What will I gain?*
> *I want to go backwards*
> *So I can begin*
> *But -*
> *The rest of my life beckons*
> *I need to win. "*
>
> *Patricia Barnett*

The law of Karma is always in existence. Karma is only the link in the chain of life. Civilisations come and go and still we learn! Contrary to what people believe, Lemuria and Atlantis were not that progressive, certainly not as progressive as the Age of Aquarius will be. The race of Lemuria based their lives on instinct and passion and therefore became extremely expansive and indulgent. The race of Atlantis allowed their higher emotions to function but used the purely rational mind to create. They became greedy, manipulative and secretive which in time created disaster. Throughout the Aquarian age humankind will evolve towards a higher consciousness of spiritual and humanitarian energies to an elevated position of universal love, compassion and truth.

These civilisations acquired knowledge from 'The Gardeners of the Earth'. However they failed to use this knowledge for creating stability and positive growth.

"Truth and knowledge do not create wisdom.
but the ability to use these traits for positive achievement,
This is wisdom!"

Evolutionary growth gives to all humanity the power to expand consciousness - to reach an expanded awareness of spiritual comprehension that is far, far, greater than any age which has gone before. Do not waste too much time on the past - learn from it but know Karma gives us all the ability to progress to a greater understanding as we continue our journey to *the light*.

Always remember - consciousness evolves.

This is the most exciting time in our evolution - for soon humanity will be able to verify these higher truths, through the knowledge given by a new divine teacher/messenger and his assistants. The time has come when we can let go of the dogma, illusion and ritual of the past. Truth will no longer be distorted - as it has in the annals of history - through the power hungry individuals who wanted to be idolised like the Gods themselves. These individuals who were here to help humanity misused their power and omitted the truth. They manipulated the masses and inevitably plunged much of humanity into darkness. This is the dawning of *the Golden Age* and very soon all religions will fall to make way for this new knowledge based on truth and love.

"Honour the person who is awake and shows us the way."

Throughout our many, many, lifetimes we will all have to eventually make a conscious effort to change, evolve, regenerate and transform to the higher realms of divine truth and perceptivity. So we always choose a life which hopefully will bring evolutionary growth and development. Of course we do not always achieve this but this is our Karmic responsibility. Believe it or not we never choose a pathway of negativity for our lives on earth. However we may have to experience negativity simply because of our past actions, patterns, attitudes, ideals and choices.

Everything in life is only a probability! Why? Because life is choice! If we have not overcome or transcended extreme negative patterns and attitudes we will journey on the path of darkness. Especially so if we cannot let go of the negative reaction of Karmic obstacles and trials, not just from our past lives but from our early formative years as well as those we create as we journey through life.

Then there are those who decide to choose the negative path in life because it is easier or in many instances it sounds so much more exciting. If we do decide to walk this negative path - for whatever reason - we create many, many, more heartaches and trials which were not included in the divine plan. This will definitely have repercussions on our future incarnations. Contrary to what many people believe it is impossible to choose a life where we come back as animals. This would not bring the possibility for any Karmic and evolutionary growth. Animals do have reincarnation but not Karma.

Judy came to me for some insight and direction. She had some problems because of the way her mother treated her when she was younger. Today she is still holding onto resentment and bitterness because she cannot forgive her mother for the treatment she received. She has been having counselling for the last six years for the very same reason. What she wanted she said, "Was for her mother to beg her forgiveness!" Her mother would not!

Karmicly there are many who are back on the earth plane to regenerate themselves through love. Not to come from their own need for love, acceptance and attachment but to give to others unconditional love through social consciousness and responsibility for their *own* regeneration. Not only to reverse their present negativity of selfishness and resentment but to transcend all past patterning and conditioning of bitterness, jealousy, spite, hate, interference, revenge and tyranny. The energies of selfishness reversed to selflessness! To care, share and love others through social interaction and responsibility. Certainly not to come from dependent or co-dependent energies or to waste their lives in useless self-sacrifice becoming martyrs in their giving and nurturing.

More often than not these individuals possess many of the 6's in their Numerology blueprint. Extreme negative 6's believe justice is an eye for an eye which will always create negative karma from one lifetime to the next. Her mother will have negativity to transcend next lifetime if she remains rigid and unbending in her outlook. For Judy her Karmic growth is not determined by her Mother's choices but her own! If Judy cannot forgive her Mother this lifetime and reach neutral ground she will have to come back with her again in a future lifetime to sort out this bitterness and resentment. "Seems very hard and cruel doesn't it?"

Many times when we experience hardships as children it is because we ourselves have created in past lives negative situations and conditions for others or for those very people we live with. Very often the lesson lies with both parties but there is always a Karmic reason why we choose such a life! These are our tests - to change, to grow, to evolve and to transform. The ability to overcome and transcend all the negativity which is created from the *misconceptions* of who we are and why we are here! These lessons apply to all of us, mothers, fathers, daughters and sons.

There are many adults who are creating extremely harsh, cruel and perverted environments for children. What will their Karma be as children or adults next lifetime or in future incarnations if they do not change their thought patterns now? Negative Karma comes to most of us through our own negative actions not just from the past but also the present. We must eventually reverse our patterning to bring balance back into our lives through positive action! This is justice. Education of course is a major catalyst for all positive change! Let go set yourselves free from the limitation and bondage which all negative emotions and attitudes create as you journey to the light.

> *"The greatest value is not in falling -*
> *but in rising again, when we do fall."*

The very first steps on the journey, 'Crossing The Barrier To The Light Of Expanded Consciousness' is the right attitudes and right thinking. This means we must choose the right aspirations backed by integrity and good behavioural patterns. Morality plays an important part in our evolution also. By looking back into history one can see great civilisations have crumbled because of negative moral codes and practices. A lot of our patterning has already been set from the past, from our previous incarnations and it will take will-power and discipline to overcome them. Knowledge of previous lifetimes and of the patterns and conditioning we have chosen to hang onto can very often provide the key for change.

What are some of the negative patterns which we find ourselves repeating over and over again which must be transcended either in this life or our future incarnations in order to gain our freedom?

Aggression, fear, guilt, need, desire, dependency, greed, jealousy, envy, hate, revenge, judgement, gossip, deceit, frivolity, laziness, violence, resentment, whining, unforgiveness, manipulation, vanity, selfishness, egotism, rigidity, bitterness, dishonesty, fanaticism, superiority, theft, cruelty - to animals or humans, pride, instability, weakness, deception, pessimism, tunnel vision, stubbornness, malice, ambition for just self, indiscretions, bad temper, tyranny - domestic or otherwise, harassment, destruction, superficiality, irresponsibility, perversion, mistaken ideals, despondency, cynicism, slavery, drudgery, sarcasm, love for power, emotionalism, moroseness, scepticism, lying, cowardice, discontent, centralisation, devilry, confusion, immoral laws and conduct - drink - drugs - sex, murder, suicide ....

All connected to the misuse and abuse of our own cosmic reality - our very lifeline - *love*. Love is the unifying and regenerative force of all life. It is the bridge between yin and yang, spirit and matter, heaven and earth. Love is the most potent of all energies. This is indeed, majestic power and therefore becomes a tremendous force for existence.

When someone asks, "What's love?" Do we include the above energies? Never - and yet they trip us up and bowl us over, many, many times. They create the deceptions and limitation in our lives. Many become imprisoned, enslaved and obsessed by these very same energies. They limit us to a life of fantasy, delusion, illusion, slavery and a great many unhealthy realities and therefore bind us Karmically to the earth plane.

Our ultimate purpose of liberation does not require us to be perfect just simply to transcend the encapsulation of physical, emotional, mental and spiritual bondage and live our lives through an expanded consciousness! A consciousness of love, truth and faith! A consciousness which encompasses more purified thoughts and deeds everyday. The mystical states of enlightenment and illumination require greater abilities which will expand our awareness to even higher dimensions of profound wisdom.

> *"We are all more than we think,*
> *but are we perfect?*
> *We must change and grow.*
> *There is a right time for this,*
> *neither too early or too late.*
> *That time is now!"*

CHAPTER 2

FEAR......... *"Most dangers are our own phantoms,*
caused by fears and illusions."

This is the largest single factor creating havoc in our lives. What is fear? Fear is born from the imagination - the mind - it is 'imaginings'.

"To live in fear, is not to live at all."
states an ancient philosophy.

Fear immobilises, it shuts down the ability to function positively so we then learn to function on another level - through negative means.

This is how all negative conditioning
and patterning is created!

Fear is created from superstition, dogma, ritual, illusion, rigidity, tunnel vision, negative patterning, possession, obsession and imagination. Some fears we may never have to deal with however, if they affect our life and the lives of others then we will definitely have to break the patterns and misconceptions for progress and development.

Many hide behind fear and this in turn limits and binds. There is no expansion with fear, it prevents us from moving on. It creates a life of limitation and bondage - it is all encompassing. It clouds our whole perception of life, of belief systems, of others and worse still, of ourselves.

It gives us excuses not to move forward and to expand. It deceives, it cheats, it grinds to a halt our evolutionary and Karmic growth to the higher planes of divine wisdom.

Every one of us has experienced fear in some shape or form. It clutches us by the throat, it torments, it creates, it visualises, it manifests, it gives birth to mental and physical diseases. It is dis-ease which creates disease!

"Fear, Superstition and Ignorance are the beginning of nightmares".

Fear is a growth, it is a cancer, it eats away at our rational mind, it is imagination gone mad. It is a seed which grows and festers. Look at your fear - *see* it, rationalise it, analyse it, dissect it, go beyond it and then transcend it. When we face our fears they do not seem as insurmountable. Share your fears with others - this then lessens the hold. You don't need to be ashamed of them and you certainly don't

Need to hang onto them like familiar friends!

Remember these are only patterns and conditioning you are hanging onto. The patterns and conditions born from the rational mind which we create from one lifetime to the next and the next. That's the illusion! We are here to transform and regenerate ourselves. There are many ways to overcome problems and blockages but first we have to recognise the problems. This is *self-awareness*! Letting go of familiar patterns is not an easy process but it eventually brings individualisation and freedom.

Letting go, is always a positive step in our lives. It develops initiative, courage, strength, empowerment and eventually leads to expanded consciousness. To break the *need* for attachment on any plane of existence means we must let go of the many fears and delusions of the physical world.

To overcome - you will become!

Fear is created from negative perceptions and therefore causes all types of behavioural problems and mental diseases over many lifetimes. Paranoia, manic depressives, fixations, obsessive disorders, schizophrenic, neurotic tendencies. So it stands to reason why we must try to break these patterns before they take hold.

We must become aware of *who we are and where we are going.* When we become aware of the *divine spirit within,* we are well on the way, not through ideals and belief systems which confine, repress and imprison but through the love and understanding which comes from expanding consciousness. This comes from the ability to control and expand our mental faculties, to think, to be rational but with extended vision.

"A rational mind is only the beginning of wisdom, it is not the end of it."

There are many, many fears in life which trip us up and bowl us over: *fear of rejection, fear of not being loved or needed, fear of letting go, fear of weakness, fear of success, fear of failure, fear of open spaces, fear of closed spaces, fear of heights, fear of the dark, fear of sickness, fear of death, fear of being alone, fear of men, fear of women, fear of sex, fear of commitment, fear of responsibility, fear of authority, fear of work, fear of confinement, fear of individualisation, fear of saying no, fear of loss, fear of God, fears, fears and more fears.*

Fear creates dependencies, co-dependencies, need and lack of belief in self. Many women live life with a Cinderella or Sleeping Beauty complex waiting for Prince Charming to wake them up and change their lives. This is asking the impossible - to be completely responsible for the happiness of another human being! Many men expect the same! Their mothers take care of their needs for part of their lives then they marry so their wives can do the same. This mentality definitely has to change! Thankfully through truth and the higher awareness which comes from Karmic and evolutionary growth, it will!

> *"Many strange Gods are worshipped and the*
> *gold fish swims round and round in its bowl.*
> *No journey is ever safe, while there is an end in view.*
> *Only the pure cease to travel, for they are not reborn.*
> *Then without fear, go!"*

Have faith and trust in who you are - love yourself - *Believe in yourself.* If you have to change - change! Progressive change always brings progress. It is what frees us - it creates the transformation and regeneration needed to help us journey into the light.

Change will always come through the development of self, physically, emotionally, mentally and spiritually. Age is no barrier! Group therapy, courses, lectures, seminars and books may be needed to help motivate and guide you on this path of growth and development. Always maintain a great deal of discrimination or you may end up more confused than when you started. Astrology and Numerology are also excellent tools for learning to know and understand self. Becoming aware of self through whatever means available or just through the many experiences of life will always expand our vision and eventually lead to a higher level of cognisance.

Many fears are manifested from *negative reactions* created from the conditions of previous lifetimes. Therefore we must all be careful not to keep repeating negative patterns but to comprehend *who we are and why we are here?* Through the many lives we experience we can learn, understand and evolve. *You* have the power - your own power - to choose.

Do not give your power away to anything or to anyone and do not create more negative patterning.

Man is energy and energy is power! Are you using this energy positively or are you negating your potential? Do you expect someone else to do it for you? Are you motivated? Are you aware? Believe in yourself! Take control of your own energies. Do not let then control you. Become empowered! *Empower Yourself!* Unconditional love for self is the first *golden rule.*

> *"A prudent man sees danger and hides himself.*
> *But the simple go on and suffer for it."*

Self-esteem comes from believing in yourself, believing in your own capabilities. Growth, development and awareness come when we perfect and develop our talents, skills and ourselves. We do not need to fear or to hang onto others for what we can give ourselves! Don't get caught up with egotism. Sometimes we like to hang onto negative patterning for sympathy or there may simply be co-dependency issues to look at.

The comedian Steady Eddy, who has cerebral palsy, once said;

> *"Sympathy is wasted on losers."*

Think about this for a moment! Sympathy creates self-pity. This is not the path to expanded consciousness! The journey to neutrality and liberation is to believe in self unconditionally but it also means we must transcend self. Sympathy creates the need to centre on self. Centralisation! The inability to see beyond! Perception then becomes clouded there is no light! Very often this creates emotional cripples! This is a journey of darkness! Replace sympathy with new thoughts, directions, ideas, ideals, attitudes and philosophies and then the empathy and understanding you want to share with others will be used for positive direction.

Lack of motivation creates obstacles, heartaches, loss and unfulfilment. What creates lack of motivation and negativity? All the guilts and fears of our rational mind, the baser needs and desires of our emotional and physical senses and ignorance!

The more we try to hide our fears the more they become real. By bringing them out into the open we can understand, conquer and transcend them. Whatever the mind perceives so we become. Fear creates stagnant conditions and the inability to move forward for growth. Self-awareness means we must expand upon the *who* and *what* we are through our ability to grasp greater depth and understanding of our inner self - our psyche. We cannot do this through fear and darkness, so therefore we must always seek the light. The need to question is always a positive step to freedom.

All negative thoughts must be restrained, transcended and transformed or they will create negative action in our lives. This awareness will always create the changes necessary for our evolutionary growth and development to a higher consciousness.

"Most dangers are our own phantoms,
caused by fears and illusions."

CHAPTER 3

NEED AND DESIRE..... *"Desires can never be satisfied,*
but they can be mastered through
awakening."

We all create need and even desire from many of our emotional frustrations and our need for attachments. There are many who fill their lives with these emotional dependencies and those who become obsessive with the needs and desires for material and physical reality.

Need is emotional frustration:

Created from the misconceptions and the inability to let go! It is the *possession* of our senses and feeds our psyche through negative means. Need and fear are just two of the energies which denies the possibility of our highest attainment - freedom and liberation from the earth plane.

Energies like fear, need and desire create negative conditions and patterns in our lives. These are the chains of illusion, repression and imprisonment which keep us earth bound. If we could control our urges - we would not need to need! Through the control of our negativity we could transcend need. Many of the needs and desires which we create in our lives are extremely transient.

Emotional need and desire creates limitation and bondage therefore it becomes imperative we break these negative patterns in this lifetime or in future incarnations. Each and every one of us has had many lives as mothers, fathers, daughters, sons and lovers to many others. So why do we need to hang on in this lifetime? When we leave the earth plane we will have created many more Karmic attachments through our many needs and desires which will have to be sorted out in future incarnations. Let go of the *need* for attachment! Love by all means - but without the self deception created from the many obsessions, desires and dependencies of our emotional energies.

Through the inability to control our emotional reasoning capabilities we fail to accept responsibility for ourselves and consequently project blame and anger onto others. So it stands to reason when we individualise - become complete within the self - we can also become empowered emotionally. This will enable our love relationships to take on new dimensions because we can love without ownership and bondage.

There are many whom we call, 'lost souls.' The souls who have passed over to the other side but who have not found the light. They live in an outer world of darkness and fog simply because of *hanging on* to the needs and desires of the physical world. There are also those who are there who do not believe in life after death. If one does not believe how does one create? The positive versus the negative, the light versus darkness.

**"We are what we believe and all that we are,
springs from our thoughts."**

Many blockages are created from abandonment and rejection. Very often these problems stem from our inner needs. 'Why has this happened to me?' Many ask. "Why was I not or why am I not needed?" To understand and comprehend this takes insight, understanding and self-awareness. If we allow these issues to take hold and stifle our growth we become imprisoned by emotional need and desire and therefore create more negative patterning in our lives. Anger, bitterness and promiscuity are perfect examples.

Therefore we are allowing these negative energies to own us! Look at the problem and realise this may be the very lesson you have chosen to overcome this lifetime. Karma was no doubt involved, it almost always is as we always choose our parents there may be unresolved issues to overcome. To realise we are *complete* within ourselves is a major stepping stone on our journey to the light of higher realisations.

For instance, if there are problems with lack of love as a child there are two choices of reaction! The first is to come from a *need* to compensate for the lack of love with the need for love, the need for attachment. The second choice is to transcend these feelings completely! To know and understand self - to love self. To *overcome* the need for compensation. *This is not what true love is anyway*! This is coming from personal needs and desires - inadequacy! The inability to love self! Remember we are here to transform, regenerate and to transcend. The ability to rise to a higher level through our *own* self-empowerment. This is the only path to wisdom!

Definitely not to fill our lives with continual unfulfilment, desolation, need and the desire to compensate for lack of being needed and loved but to expand consciousness through the ability *to focus on new ideas for creating positive growth and development.* While we search for and need love we will always be bound to the continual rounds of life, death and rebirth and to this world of attachments, needs and desires.

This then is our power - the power of one! The ability to overcome to become! If the problem has been created in this lifetime only then it must still eventually be sorted out. Remember we will always reap what we sow. Transcending need is an extremely important lesson for Karmic and evolutionary growth. With abandonment issues perhaps the problem belongs to the other person, it may be their Karmic lesson. Try to understand this. Understanding brings acceptance and acceptance brings peace. Change your perception and let your needs go - do not become enslaved by them - transcend them. Take control - *Nurture yourself - love yourself - empower yourself.*

As the famous and beautiful," Desiderata" says:

"You are a child of the universe,
no less than the trees and the stars;
you have a right to be here."

Believe in yourself unconditionally - not because you were loved and accepted but because you are you! A beautiful, creative and talented individual. You are here to evolve, to transform, to transcend and to learn through the development of self. There are many who have chosen to learn this very powerful lesson this lifetime. The lesson of detachment

- the transcendence of emotional reasoning ability and bondage to our inner needs and desires. It is through this pathway we get caught up with the negative emotions of bitterness, resentment, spite, hate and guilt.

All these needs and desires belong to physical reality. In the higher scheme of things they do not matter. What matters is we must eventually *overcome* all physical, emotional, mental and spiritual bondage. This is the path which eventually leads to wisdom, neutrality, illumination and liberation. Wake up - penetrate this world of illusion - the world of personal desires and emotional needs which chain us to the perpetual cycle of life, death and rebirth.

My belief is there are more blockages caused from the needs we create in our lives than from anything else. Men and women put their lives on hold because of need. They feel they are nothing until they have someone to love or need. Need creates the blockages which prevent us from recognising our creative potential and denies the implementation of our Karmic obligations and evolutionary growth.

We can never empower ourselves through this attitude. The need for mothering - to be taken care of - comes from fear and prevents us from moving forward. Mother yourself - love yourself - empower yourself, through your own strength and courage. Unconditional love for self will cancel all negativity and bring more protection than anything else. Faith can move mountains - that is faith in self.

Many experience unfulfilment and desolation through the many negative patterns and conditions in their lives. They do not know who they are or where they are going. This has the ability to create tremendous blockages but the positive aspect of this realisation is it eventually initiates the need to question and then to *seek and find*. This in turn instigates the need for change and positive change always brings progress.

There are many individuals who desperately seek a partner. What a great many of these men and women do not understand is they are here to balance all existence through positive energies. This is what balance means. Not just to balance their lives with a mate on an emotional plane but to balance their whole lives through their physical, mental and spiritual energies. This is balance - self-empowerment on all levels of existence! To focus on developing their creative and spiritual energies to a more advanced stage of awareness. This is evolutionary growth! This then enables us all to care and love through a more practical reasoning facility. One which does not focus just on the personal self but manifests love and understanding through social consciousness, then social responsibilities.

The ability to reverse all manipulative, cruel and selfish behaviour into deeds of kindness and responsibility which are established through loving and helping others. The reversal of selfishness to selflessness! Loving, caring and giving unconditionally from the heart with detachment will certainly bring positive growth and development on the journey to the light. Love then encompasses a much higher and purer realm of compassion, tolerance and truth.

"The wise seek to journey through truth and light,
The fool, through the gratification of
his own needs and desires."

Another example of need creating blockages over many lifetimes is the following:

A friend of mine had the ability to access several lifetimes where she had known and loved a certain man. For karmic reasons they had not actually been able to perpetuate this love because of accidental and sudden death. In the lifetimes when this man left her life through his death she had always collapsed on her emotions. She had never realised or achieved her obvious potential because of the need she had for him and her subsequent loss.

This lifetime they met once more and she fell madly in love with him. " Have we met before?" he asked. A casual friendship was established but again the pattern was repeated and he went out of her life. Not through death but with no further recognition or intimate sharing. What she had not realised was she had chosen this painful lesson again this lifetime. The lesson - not to collapse emotionally every time he left her life!

This woman is a visionary, extremely gifted and talented and had never pursued her ideals further. Now she has realised why she had to let go and empower herself for her own individualisation - her own achievement. When she does this perhaps then she will be ready for another special and beautiful relationship based on equality, respect, and honour and not on emotional need. Letting go of patterns and attitudes created from need in previous lives is very often painful and distressing but is essential for our Karmic and evolutionary development. This lesson of *letting go* is one which many of us choose for growth on the journey to the light.

The ability to transcend need will only come from our own *individualisation.* The lesson of complete belief in self can be extremely difficult but necessary for the liberation of being corded to people, things and emotional hunger on the earth plane. While we experience hate and intense love we are Karmicly corded to the individuals involved. Neutrality is what we have to achieve and through this we break the chains which bind. Love can still be shared but the love which has transcended the purely emotional level and the *need* for attachment.

"The dreamer usually thinks he is awake."

Some religions believe in freedom of mind and spirit but many come from religious dogma and suppression. This inhibits growth. Again this will have to be overcome in this lifetime or in future incarnations.

Our purpose here is to free ourselves from all rigid thought patterns which in turn frees the spirit. To become enslaved by people, ideas, belief systems, patterning and conditioning is restraint of individuality and freedom of our very mind and soul. We *must all use* discrimination, discipline, truth and love to achieve this exalted state and then we too can expand our spiritual horizons.

The following quote most of us have seen at one time or another:

"If you love something, set it free,
If it returns, it's yours
and if it doesn't,
** it never was!**

Then, there is this version which I have seen which seems to be written especially for those who allow their needs and desires to become obsessive.

> ***"If you love something, set it free,***
> ***If it returns, it's yours,***
> ***and if it doesn't hunt it down and kill it!***

I think *most* of us can laugh at this but many people do allow their needs and desires to completely possess them and they cannot *see*. Their perception becomes distorted and the mind is blinded with illusions, delusions and deception. Change your focus from self absorption and centralisation to looking outside yourself. Learn to love the self but also expand your vision to encompass not only the many wonders of nature but the true significance and reality of life. Cultivate knowledge and creativity then the love you do have can be extended to all humankind and not just to the personal self. Higher consciousness will always bring the ability to *love self* - then to *transcend self*!

So through the trials, heartaches, loss and unfulfilment of life we experience a crucifixion which helps us understand an extremely valuable and beautiful lesson. The need to let go of self, of egotism and of need. When we focus only on ourselves, on our own needs and desires we actually lose our power. Because when we come from egocentric energies we create many undesirable fantasies. This in turn produces more negative patterning, conditioning and even sickness which must eventually be overcome.

The need for physical and emotional gratification will never bring complete happiness simply because when we concentrate on need and desire we negate the growth of the spirit. We are one tenth conscious and only nine tenths subconscious, which means our higher self reigns supreme. Therefore if we have not overcome or transcended the emotional, mental, physical and spiritual frustrations in our lives unfulfilment will be the end result. We seem to think once our physical and emotional needs have been realised we are going to live happily ever after.

This will never happen if we negate our Karmic and evolutionary growth. Many fill their lives with misconceptions and live in a delusional world of make believe. Their whole perception and existence consists of the very energies which bring them limitation and bondage to the earth plane. The most powerful and degenerative of all these energies are the needs and desires which chain us to an exaggerated physical existence - a life of phantasmal reality.

Eventually one has to penetrate this *World of Illusion* either this lifetime or in future incarnations. Emotional needs have to be transcended to find individualisation, the completeness of self. This is the only pathway to neutrality and freedom. *Emotional need* is an extremely negative ego energy.

The need for countless possessions to find happiness and fulfilment is also a very transient and superficial life! Beautiful things are fine as long as we know that is all they are, a false perspective of physical reality and we do not worship or cling to them. To do so is still attachment to physical impermanence. Remember they do not provide happiness, expanded consciousness, neutrality or liberation from this world of entrapments.

Why is it we never see what we *do* have but always see what we *don't* have! Do you realise this is why there are certain things in life we are denied? These are our tests! The tests and lessons we have to *overcome* to transcend the physical world. Do we see and expand upon who we are or are we looking and trying to find someone or something else for our *completeness*? We are here to achieve on all levels to attain higher awareness and freedom from this world of illusion, this world of negative encapsulation.

When we expand our consciousness and use our power to overcome to become; to achieve and to uplift; to always encompass others and humanity we empower ourselves and this gives others the motivation to become empowered.

> *"The teaching of the wise*
> *is a fountain of life,*
> *that one may avoid*
> *the snares of death."*

If we *need* love we are failing to love ourselves. How can love bloom and grow stronger if we cannot love the self unconditionally? To expect love from others when we fail to love the self is very hypocritical and fraudulent. It is living a lie. It is virtually saying, "Will you please love me unconditionally? I need love, all your love desperately (always a word to watch). You must give me all your love and time because I won't be whole if you don't".

In other words "I don't know who I am so I need your love to give me strength, courage, self-esteem and support. I need to own you because I can't own or respect myself. I can't love myself therefore I need someone else to love and for them to love me. Without you I can't empower myself." This very problem is evident to the extreme in the many cases of individuals who kill their partners or children and then kill themselves. This is certainly negative patterning not being overcome. This will create more Karmic conditions which will have to be resolved in future lifetimes. To love self unconditionally is the first step to self-awareness.

"If you want recognition, recognise yourself."

To reach 'The Light Of Expanded Consciousness,' we must be willing to transform ourselves. We are all on the *stairway to heaven* - the immortality of the spirit from baser physical reality. The journey of many lifetimes to end the cycle of life, death and rebirth. Baser needs and desires have no part on this journey to freedom.

All negativity is created from the many needs and desires of the physical dimension. These are manifested simply through our perception of right and wrong, light and darkness, truth and illusion and all our negative ego energies. Many come just from the inability to say, 'no.' This can then create denial of the laws of decency, morality, honesty and integrity. Our journey is to the light of divine wisdom therefore we must become empowered through positive means.

All needs and desires belong to a transient world. We still have the opportunity to *use* physical manifestations for higher achievement - but to know and understand this is all it is! The reality of a purely physical existence! Do not delude yourself - in the higher scheme of things this is all an illusion! Physical reality of the physical world is *not* immortality of the spirit from the earth plane.

> ***"You are your only master. To straighten the crooked, you must straighten yourself"***

Jan and Michael came to me for their Numerology charts. After I had finished discussing them I asked if there were any questions? The couple wanted to know what I thought of their plans for the future? This vibrant lovely woman could not fall pregnant and they wanted to go back to their country of origin to live. There she had a sister who was willing to become a surrogate mother for her. I thought this over for awhile - looked at her chart and saw the answers. Part of her lesson this lifetime was to overcome her emotional reasoning ability and to expand and pursue her creativity for the upliftment of others. This is a valuable spiritual lesson for Karmic and evolutionary growth. Many of us have severe tests to master this and many fail. To tame the animal nature (our needs and desires) and to transcend the needs of self. She was not to collapse on her emotions but to look to what she already possessed and use these abilities for progress. Not to focus on what she did not or could not have.

This lifetime she had chosen to individualise - to achieve her highest potential on a creative level and to let go of her emotional need and desire for mothering! This was still her choice and certainly Karmic. An extremely difficult lesson! When I finished explaining the reasons why she had chosen these obstacles she seemed to feel much more relaxed and free.

Need will always trip us up and bowl us over and fill our lives with longing, unfulfilment, heartache and undesirable realities. *Need is an illusion and emotion is the net!* Through the creation and recreation of needs and desires many lose direction for the implementation of their Karmic purpose and their very own evolutionary growth and development.

Numerologically speaking need vibrates to the 19/1. To the grave and back - to death and back. This is the number of surrender which is what need is - surrendering ourselves to the continual cycle of life, death and rebirth. If negative which emotional need is, it scorches and burns all those who come within close proximity of its' energies. It is self at all costs!

We all want to succeed in life and motivation is the key ingredient for success. But what is success? What happens when you get there and there is no *there*? This is why it is so important to develop the inner self to expand consciousness. This creates the freedom which comes from letting go of the needs and desires of the illusory world. Certainly not to negate achievement but to know and discriminate between what is real and lasting - between the true and the false. The ability to achieve positively on all plains of existence brings wisdom which in turn brings neutrality and neutrality brings liberation.

"What is wasting a life?
By chasing material and illusory things.
What is a life that is not wasted?
One where we learn a little."

CHAPTER 4

LOVE........ "*We should never allow ourselves,*

to become "enslaved by love".

Love should never be confused with *need*. Think about this for a moment. We think we need someone to love. "We need love". "I can't live without love". "My life is nothing now he/she has gone". How many times have you heard these comments perhaps even said them yourself, not just about the love interest in your life but even children who have left home or our loved ones who have departed to *the other side.* Attachment can very often be mistaken for love. Need and attachment can sometimes be unhealthy. Fantasies and misconceptions are created from our needs and desires. Many times these negative energies manifest a false perspective in our lives and will continue until we change our perceptions and attitudes. For many, many individuals love is created through personal need more than from genuine affection and caring for the other person.

Love is not egotism, it is not dependency, it is not need, it is not a desire, it is not delusion, it is not a fantasy, it is not a habit, it is not a duty, it is not guilt, it is not fear, it is not a crutch, it is not obsession or ownership therefore it should not imprison or stifle us. It is unconditional, it is acceptance, it is joy, it is energy and it is unity.

Love should never bring limitation and bondage into our lives. *Love is regeneration* - so it should lift us up to a higher consciousness. Love encompasses life itself. Love conquers hate. Love conquers loneliness. This is not just the love between man and woman but the love for everyone - for friends, for family and for humanity.

> **"Love builds, it creates, it warms, it regenerates,**
> **it transforms, it beautifies,**
> **it expands, it transcends, it inspires, it heals,**
> **it nourishes, it unites, it cares and it empowers."**

There are many kinds of loving and they normally fall into two categories, the personal and the humanitarian. As the name suggests personal love deals with *love for the self*. Whether we give it or receive it, it is still love for or from the self. This is the love which brings attachment. It is the love which is associated with our own emotional needs. Basing all life on love for just the self is very confined, limiting and selfish. We must extend our love and divine compassion to encompass all humanity.

Many search for their perfect love or their soul mate. This may never be realised simply because of Karma. There are many who have chosen to learn this extremely important lesson of individualisation and sometimes this cannot be achieved with a partner. To believe in self unconditionally is to transcend self! Therefore Karmicly this lifetime we may have to extend our vision to encompass and serve others instead. To develop our own creativity for the upliftment of humanity or simply to achieve higher spiritual reality. It does not matter in what capacity we achieve, we are still here to learn to let go of the personal *need* for attachment!

No self-sacrifice or martyrdom is required. Love and service for others gives us all the ability to *transcend self!* Giving to humanity will always produce positive Karma whether we have personal love or not. Very often pesonal love can be created through our own *expectations of love* - in love with love! This is illusion and fantasy.

The ability to empower self without the need for a relationship certainly may not be an easy lesson to learn but once mastered it's reward can be far more precious than the *need* for attachment. Being on one's own is almost classed as one of the deadly sins. It is not! It may be one of the most valuable and progressive lessons of all - *individualisation.*

There are many Karmic choices made by all of us for each and every lifetime. These will help guide and motivate us to extend our vision and expand our awareness to higher realms of understanding for our eventual liberation from the earth plane. *Letting go* throughout life is often stressful and agonising. For many it is a necessary spiritual and evolutionary experience. There are numerous ways of learning this painful but necessary lesson of nonattachment. I have known families who are virtually forced apart, many who have had to leave their countries of birth, separations, divorce, sickness, death of loved ones - babies and children - all to teach *the letting go process.*

To believe in self - to individualise - to be complete within the self - to empower self - to learn acceptance - to have faith - to transcend all physical manifestations - to love humanity and to gain our freedom and liberation for the immortality of our spirit. These are the *real* reasons for our existence on the earth plain. While many *hang on* and *need others,* they fail to individualise and this brings limitation and bondage

- they are bound by others - by people and feelings. This in turn is imprisonment to the physical world.

> *"There are those who give and those who take.*
> *Both extremes are wrong.*
> *Wisdom, life, the very secrets of the*
> *universe, are natural - in the golden middle way.*
> *The martyr has gone too far and will not find peace*
> *except in death and the chance to try again.*
> *The ruthlessly selfish, are the stuff of monsters."*

Individualisation is not isolation - it is not cutting oneself off from humanity. It is thinking and acting independently - to take responsibility for self and for the individual choices one makes. This does not mean we cannot interact with others. We all need to live in an interdependent world. Humanity interconnects therefore it must communicate and live together. This is the law of nature and of all the universe. To do this successfully we must all nurture divine compassion and love for everyone. These are the *golden cords* - the cords that free.

> *"Those who care, will be cared for."*

There is so much depression, heartache and mental sickness created from loneliness. Loneliness is not only created from the inability to freely give love and divine compassion to others but very often from the inability to love the self. This in turn inhibits many from developing their very important social skills. Unbelievable as it many sound, loneliness has almost become a disease (dis-ease) in today's society.

We must all learn to let go of fear, all negative perceptions and the need to give to others motivated by our own needs and desires. As I have said before fear will always destroy our senses and create darkness in our conscious and subconscious existence.

Then there are those who have totally given themselves in sacrifice and martyrdom to their children. Many men have devoted their lives to their work and have not developed their creative abilities and in many cases their social expertise. Each and everyone of us is responsible for who we are so it is up to us to develop all our talents, friendships and ourselves.

"The simple believes everything,
but the prudent looks where he is going."

All our anguish, pain, heartaches and unfulfillment will eventually bring the ability to penetrate this ambiguous world. Not only to learn acceptance but to change our attitudes, our belief systems and ourselves. Then and only then does life become more tranquil, peaceful and progressive. Acceptance then awareness brings expansion and the ability to go beyond.

The first and foremost rule of love is love for self. Do you believe in yourself? Can you honestly say, "I believe in myself?" Say it to yourself - over and over again! We must all learn to love and believe in ourselves. If everyone could believe in self (not from egotism or humility - but with innocence) we could all let go of many of the negative energies which emanate from the desperate need for attachment.

●

Humility is a word which has brought with it guilt, repression, fear and rejection of self over many lifetimes. It was as if without humility we were committing a deadly sin. To believe in ourselves we empower ourselves! This is not wrong! Over many lifetimes through guilt and religious dogma there have been those who have been tormented and tortured because they allowed themselves the privilege of ego - and then thought this was wrong.

What is ego? It is self, motive, force, id, collective unconscious, inner space, pre-conscious, subconsciousness.

It is *egotism* which is negative! So what is egotism? It is egomania, narcissism, self-absorption, self-indulgence, hoggishness, possessiveness, opportunism, sordidness, inconsideration, mercenary, bludger, self-seeking. So of course it becomes apparent why we must all let go of egotism. To believe in self is positive energy! *To thine own self be true.* Faith can move mountains - that is faith in self. We certainly must as the Bible suggests, *become like children* not through humility which is self defeating but through *purity and innocence.*

Therefore if we could all teach our children and grandchildren to love themselves we would be well on the way. Education is the catalyst for change. Cruel parenting is another pattern which is usually related to past life circumstances. To break the patterning takes understanding and education.

> ***Teach - Do not condemn...***
> ***Ignorance is the root of all evil.***

When we become complete within the self we have the ability to let go of many 'hang ups' and prejudices. Loving self brings the ability to say *'no'*. Do you know it means, *freedom and upliftment?* Love begins with the self - this is our power. This then gives us the ability for love within the family. Happy loving families create stable and happy communities and happy communities make a happy world.

Children who do not receive love can still transcend many obstacles if they learn to love and believe in self. Denial of love does not necessarily make a victim but lack of love for self very often does. It does not matter how many times an individual is told he/she is loved they may not hear if they have brought back inner guilt from previous lifetimes. It is the love for self they have to learn, understand and accept.

"What is newly born is innocent and it needs to become aware. Simplicity and awareness should lead to clarity."

Create the power - the power of one - your own power. No matter how difficult, traumatic and unstable life is you will eventually 'overcome to become' if you love and believe in yourself unconditionally.

Cancer is created over many lifetimes from the lack of love for self. Eating away at the self! No self worth! Knowledge brings the ability to break down the barriers of conditioning and patterning of past, present and future lifetimes.

Heart attacks come to those who cannot express love. They have not yet learnt to break down the barriers of rigidity formed again from conditions and patterns created from previous incarnations. These individuals very often become workacholics as their substitute for *loving*. They must learn to use the heart centre - to expand, to be able to *give and receive love*. Holding onto guilt, rigid thought patterns, belief systems and negative energies brings many limitations into our lives especially disease. (dis-ease) In fact many heart patients cannot say, "I love you" because of the blockages caused by negative patterning and conditioning.

Physical deformities from birth are the Karmic reaction or manifestation from the continual patterning of physical gratification over many lifetimes. In other words, the abuse of the physical senses to a life of physical seduction. The saturation with physical pleasures! The inability to use and develop the mind for change and progress to higher ideals. The negative conditions they encounter this lifetime will purify these individuals for the continuation of their Karmic and evolutionary journey in future lifetimes.

To find cures for the physical manifestation of many diseases we must look to and investigate what we are using in our consumer society. The need for the use of chemicals in our world must be questioned! Greed and power has replaced truth in humankind's approach to life. We will never change the health of humanity or our environment with chemicals! Very soon humanity will have the opportunity to change consciousness, with the cataclysmic events which will overtake humankind. The Karmic and evolutionary wheel keeps turning and we keep turning with it. These changes will hopefully create new ideals, structures, ideas, attitudes and philosophies based on truth, love and divine compassion *not* on greed, power, deception and fraud!

Love is an extremely powerful weapon in fact it is one of the most powerful weapons there is. Love and belief in self does away with the need for protection and cancels all negativity. It expands the consciousness for higher growth and development and is our safety net not only this lifetime but through all future incarnations. Teaching others to believe in themselves without egocentricity can be achieved if they are taught not only to love and develop self but to love and serve humanity. *All humanity*! Selfishness reversed to selflessness!

Normally egotism is an indication of lack of positive belief in self - a need to be recognised. Loving self is knowing self! To know and understand there may be many times in our lives when we have to be alone without attachments but because we are *complete* we are never lonely.

Loving someone else does not require *saving* them. Each and everyone of us is responsible for our own lives. This is Karma.

An Ancient Eastern Philosophy:

"Love is not a crutch for cripples to lean upon!"

Personal Love   - *"Loving another is acceptance,*
it is not ownership."

The love we all think we so desperately need to be complete is an illusion! This is the need and desire for attachment. The nightmares, fears, loneliness, heartaches, longing, dependency, obsessions, possession and hanging on which men/women experience because of *need*. These emotions are not love! These intense, negative emotions, bind us to the earth plane. Two little stories to illustrate:

E. G. 1...... Many years ago I had decided to do some voluntary work at a hospital which catered for terminally ill male and female patients. As it was only a ten minute walk from where I lived I would often sit and talk to one of the female patients before I went home. One day she remarked she had an unusual visitor the night before. I did not find this surprising as her family visited her regularly. This visitor she went onto explain, was her departed husband. He had come to ask, "How long are you going to be here"? "I miss you and need you!" She said she felt it would not be long before she joined him. As it happened she only lived another 6 months!

E. G. 2...... A client was driving along in her car one day and her departed father whom she said was a very selfish man 'appeared.' She was surprised to say the least but this turned to utter astonishment when he proceeded to say, "I want your mother, I need her!" My client answered very quickly and defiantly, "Well you're not having her!"

"What is wrong with this?" you might ask. "Is this not love"? This is the love, need, attachment, dependency and ownership which binds us to baser reality. These examples illustrate perfectly what these emotions can do even after we have left the earth plane. These men may have loved their wives but they also became needy. They might have been assertive even aggressive but they had not learnt the true meaning of *individualisation*. 'Completeness of self!' This is not surprising as many men have had women look after them all their lives. First their mothers - then their wives! This is need and dependency taken beyond the earth plane. What we take with us to the other side we bring back in the next life or future lives to overcome.

"Of all Loves, the first love is self.
Until you learn to love yourself
you cannot learn to love another."

Throughout the ages most men have had mothers to take care of them (In some cases not very well, which suggest a Karmic link and lessons to be learned through the association) The very foundations of humanity are crumbling. Men and women are abusing and using their very lifeline - *love* - negatively. They are failing to empower themselves. Many men have treated women like possessions and this is the reason why women are changing.

This is why men are bewildered and lost, they don't understand what is happening. The consciousness of women must change to bring about equality. These changes are the catalyst to expand man's own consciousness! Why? Simply because women are inner reality and men are outer reality! Of course women do not have to become aggressive but they do have to become empowered! For many men this creates disorientation, turmoil and panic. There are men who actually leave their wives for other men!

When women change men become threatened, confused and fearful. Women have always taken care of their needs without too much resistance over many lifetimes. First mothers - then wives and for men the very foundation of society is disintergrating. This brings conflict. Some do not want to change and others do not know how to change. The laws of the Universe do not change! It is mass consciousness which must change whether it brings upheaval or not. This is evolutionary growth! This is Karma!

Through this 'new movement' for women there are many men who really believe their power has been taken from them and feel they aren't in charge anymore. This relates to past conditioning and patterning from Karma, religious dogma, tunnel vision, rigid thought patterns, culture and tradition. The foundation of *this* mentality should be rocked if they think they need to be in charge of anyone except themselves! This is the conflict. This is why there is so much confusion. The role of women must change for equality and evolutionary growth and therefore men will seek to reform themselves also.

When men take charge they become the *masters*. With women being the servants. (Masters always have servants) This is not power. Men have *not empowered themselves* through positive means. Through this attitude they are using and abusing the power of others especially women.

When we become empowered, we then use
our own power for our own regeneration.

Many men don't know who they are simply because they don't want to change. For thousands of years they have been *in charge*. They have been brought up with this attitude. For generations men have been able to dictate, manipulate, expect, be obeyed and own others. Suddenly many women want to know "who they are as individuals" and so have started to empower themselves. Men have become fearful because they think women have become aggressive. Perhaps some have but what has really happened is women have started to *think* not just feel! The majority of men are used to women being subservient and the changes are traumatic.

The familiar structures, systems and conditioning have started to crumble and fall apart. This will eventually create the need for change to man's own consciousness. There is no need for disillusionment and fear as men can empower themselves through new ideals, ideas, attitudes, philosophies, structures, patterns and conditions. A much more positive and expansive attitude is needed to bring equality and happiness to all.

When we refuse to understand and abuse those of the opposite sex there will always be retribution. This is why most of us have had at least one life as men *and* women - to help us understand one another on a much more positive level. Does it really matter whether we are male or female? The divine laws of truth, love, decency, integrity and morality are always in existence. This is Karma!

When we find the completeness and balance of self we do not need to be waited on, served, or obeyed. We give and take. We are all equal! We all have our own power so there is no reason to abuse or negate someone else's for our own use. Men give away their power as much as women but in many different ways. Not only through aggression, fear, guilt, sexual promiscuity, need, tyranny and abuse, but manipulation, selfishness, obsessive behaviour and egotism. We cannot empower ourselves through negative means!

These are chains of illusion and delusion and will always create negative patterning. This is certainly *not freedom!* It is limitation and bondage to our baser *ego* energies. When we pass over to "the other side" we will take with us the conscious thought patterns we leave with then bring them back with us into the next lifetime to consciously resolve.

***Self-empowerment does not mean taking charge of others,
It means taking charge of yourself.***

For many women fear and guilt have been their constant companions! This is why it is so difficult for the majority of women. They are the home makers and mothers! They care for, heal, nurture, give and love but many put themselves into bondage and servitude. Therefore they must learn to empower themselves first! This will enable them to rise to a higher position of love, respect and honour. In the future the majority of women will be respected for their knowledge, healing and power, because they themselves will be empowered. This will then give them the ability to enlighten, illuminate, educate and love through a higher realm of consciousness.

Women have intuitive strength and power - they are the heart. Men possess physical strength as well as practical and rational reasoning ability. Each can learn from one another and when we develop both our masculine and feminine attributes we will have balance. Balance within self - creates balance without. This in turn brings peace and harmony to all humankind. There will always be differences and that's the way it should be so we must try to understand and accept these differences not condemn them.

"What we do - we do to ourselves.
Some are trapped by their feelings."

So many women sacrifice their *individuality* for someone else. What they are doing is simply giving their power away because of fear, guilt, need and duty or because they think they are expressing love. Our first duty is to ourselves. *To thine own self be true.* This then gives us the opportunity to operate from a higher reality which is essential for all evolutionary development.

What are we actually on the earth plane for? We are here to transcend all negative energies to eventually 'overcome to become'. To penetrate this world of illusion to find the truth and use it.

"Truly knowing and loving yourself,
your very inner being, brings expansion
of the mind and an awareness of higher
truths and your guiding light to higher
spiritual consciousness."

Once we empower ourselves how can others take away our power? Empowerment is strength, physically, emotionally, mentally and spiritually. It is a positive belief in self! It is faith! It expands our consciousness - it regenerates and transforms. It makes possible new ideals, new ideas, new attitudes, new goals, new directions and evolutionary growth not just for self but for all civilisation.

We do not have to prove who we are
through negative means, because we
know who we are, through truth and love.

The pathway now becomes more tranquil because of more insight, balance, harmony and peace within - as we continue our journey towards the light through love and acceptance.

These changes for humanity will not happen overnight but they will happen eventually for stability, harmony, balance and peace which is really what equality is all about. Without equality between the sexes how can we create equality for all humankind? If you look around you there are subtle changes already in place. Those men who are already aware and have empowered themselves positively are the teachers of todays youth and can also change the consciousness of other men.

"Who does the chasing in a relationship if women empower themselves?" asked, a friend. Men of course, not because they are superior or the masters but just because they are men. Just like women will always *give birth*, simply because they are women. Man is outer reality and woman is inner reality. Equality gives both the ability to recognise the differences and to become empowered by them. There will always be those men who like to be chased but they are the exception not the rule. Very often these men are the one's who do not like to take responsibility for a relationship. The relationship is then created from *the woman's need.* This can be a very manipulative decoy and very often creates promiscuity!

Numerologically, *man* vibrates to 10/1. This is individualisation. A leader with a spiritual responsibility - to bring people together in peace, or to bring peace to people.' Man' has a soul of 1 - Individualisation, action, ego, concentration of the will, initiative, courage, creation, pioneer. The outer self is the 9 - The humanitarian, universal love, healing, caring, compassionate, giving and creativity - it is the universal guardian.

Negatively: 1 is aggression, egotism, arrogance, fear, dependence, tyranny, weakness, stubbornness, selfishness, cruelty and laziness. Negatively, many 9's think they are the world's great lovers. They are fickle, indiscreet, immoral, emotional, vulgar and bitter They have to transcend all these negative energies to find their freedom. 9 is death and rebirth - to let go of egotism or personal self for others. It is the love and divine compassion for all humanity.

What has happened then? 1 energies have to learn to rise above egotism and aggression. To believe in self but to transcend self. When used positively with the 9 energies of love, understanding and compassion, *man* can create a perfect balance for himself and for all humankind.

Equality is on the way. Dependency is being replaced by individuality, which is really responsibility for the self. Positive self-empowerment!

Once we become empowered we do not need to rely on anyone else to save us or to need others for emotional gratification and self-esteem. Through a positive belief in self we become motivated and then we do not need to become enslaved by need, desire or love.

There are many individuals who actually have to come back to the earth plane to learn how to love others without selfishness and dependency. Not only to give, share, nurture and understand but to learn to accept responsibility for commitment. They are here to reverse their previous negative energies into positive ones of unity, balance and harmony. Being able to accept and love others brings balance to those who have failed these responsibilities in previous incarnations.

Many fail these very important lessons because they still come from their own needs and desires - to be admired, loved and mothered and for others, from their manipulative and aggressive energies.

> *"Love is natural - give and take.*
> *Sometimes we love because of the*
> *other persons need for it.*
> *It is not the same as love which is mutual.*
> *No-one should hog all the giving or all the taking.*
> *The good - is the golden middle way."*

Ancient Buddhist Philosophy

Love is regeneration so therefore loving someone who drags you down, abuses you, enslaves you, defeats you in anyway or just simply isn't on the 'same wave length,' is self-defeating and no one benefits. Perhaps it's time to move on without criticism, judgment or bitterness..

> *"The love which fears ebb and flow - is jealousy."*

We must realise when staying in relationships which have outlived their purpose because of fear, guilt, dependency and co-dependency prevents us from individualisation and emotional empowerment. For some it takes a tremendous amount of courage to go it alone. Karma sometimes has a funny way of seeing justice done and therefore we should never judge others. Perhaps we have trodden that very same path ourselves if not this lifetime then in previous incarnations. In the 'higher scheme of things' time is irrelevant. Civilisations come and go and still we learn. Karma is always in evidence.

"Feelings are sometimes better than thought.
Feelings are important and it is wrong to neglect them.
But feelings are only a part of us.
They must be mastered,
or 'the tail will wag the dog'."

Commitment   *"A word given, should be kept.*
                      Love is no excuse to break it.
                      With love, it should be an extra
                      positive thing."

Marriage, relationships, children and work, - are some of the commitments we will encounter throughout our lives. Marriage or any personal relationship is unity - it is not bondage, enslavement or duty. Consequently we should always maintain our own individuality. It is definitely a responsibility to a commitment!

I always think a relationship is very similar to the links in a chain. There are many sorts of chains. There are those which are so meshed together, there are no spaces between the links. This kind of relationship will eventually suffocate the individuals involved. The chain I like the best is the one where there is a healthy space between the links which still come together but are separate and individual. There is no chance of becoming suffocated within this kind of relationship. The chain is intertwined but separate.

"To get respect, you have to earn it."

Most of us know love should be unconditional but what about the love we share in a relationship? A relationship is a partnership. Unless we have reached a higher realm of love consciousness or the spiritual level of neutrality, partnerships must have boundaries. If we cannot take responsibility for who we are how can we expect others to do the same. We do not have to be perfect but we are all here to work towards a higher consciousness and to transform all our negative energies into positive ones even in relationships.

Why many relationships fail is because when individuals become attached they think they have actually reached the final accomplishment in life consequently they resort to any behavioural patterning they want and so stop growing. Eventually they wonder why their relationship has floundered. Throughout any relationship and partnership we must all give and take but definitely not at the price of forfeiting self- respect. Unrealistic expectations of love are an illusion and invaribly create disappointment and heartache.

Many of our relationships are based on Karmic returns, for learning - for transforming and for transcending all negativity. Any extreme is wrong - no matter who creates it. The only way is the middle way! This is balance! Commitment means there must be rules and boundaries - or there would not be any need for accountability or the need to honour the partnership in the first place.

It is only when we reach neutrality or enlightenment we can go beyond boundaries as this is a stage of purity - purity of mind, heart and deed! Those individuals who have progressed this far would not use their personal needs, desires or baser energies to compromise or manipulate others in any situation.

I am continually being asked," What are soul mates?" I really do think the majority of individuals hang on to this illusion for a happy ever after romantic fairytale fantasy. Soul mates are individuals who come together because of Karma. It is a union through love of the physical, emotional, mental and spiritual planes within each person. Certainly not just a physical and emotional bonding. But remember this is not necessarily all that there is to our evolutionary and Karmic growth. We must all be aware we are on a journey to freedom - of detachment! To love by all means but through a higher realisation of love consciousness. It sounds special when we say *soul mate* but very often it is only Karma being played out! Karma - the law of cause and effect - from one life to the next, to the next and the next.

Numerologically - *Woman* vibrates to 21/3. The light of life which lightens the paths of many through service, love, beauty, hope, optimism, faith, kindness, creativity and happiness. It brings success and recognition in the fullness of time. It is "The Crown of Magi," it is Cosmic Consciousness which can be achieved through the mastery of self over the environment. 3 is inner reality - and when expanded upon becomes outer reality. 3 is the light of the spirit. It is growth, self-expression and acceptance. The soul of woman is the 7. The conquest on the mental plane and the ability to go within and find the seeds of life. The outer personality is 14/5. This is the 'Scribe'. Mental discernment versus physical pleasure. To overcome to become - the teacher the adept. This vibration is one of knowledge.

Negatively, these energies are not only gossip, frivolity, whining, criticism, vanity, exaggeration, silly pride, jealousy and superficiality but hypocrisy, depression, stress, scattering of energies, complacency, manipulation, extravagance and physical indulgence.

The reason women find it so hard to empower themselves is because they nurture, love, serve and give so generously. 3 is an emotional energy and a very expansive vibration. When a woman makes the comment," I'm trying to find myself," everyone thinks she has gone stark raving mad! She must find herself to empower herself! To let go of *her* extreme negative energies - the energies which limit and bind her to physical reality! Mass consciousness must change eventually and women can be the catalyst for the changes which heralds our new age.

This means throughout the 21 st. Century women will rise in stature and power and be recognised and respected as equals. This does not mean women should trample men in the attempt! Women will obtain equality when they stop giving their power away because of need, dependency, fear, guilt and manipulation. Women must say *no*! Enough is enough! It is time to stop the conditioning and patterning of the past. It is time to change the rigid belief systems of a male dominated society. (Patriarchy) This certainly does not mean we have to have a female dominated society. (Matriarchy) One is as bad as the other. All we need is *equality*! This new consciousness for women is actually documented in the Bible.

Mass consciousness has to change and women will no longer be treated as second class citizens. Throughout the history of the world men have sought power to dominate and therefore women have used their power to manipulate. New ideals and philosophies will create greater respect, understanding and expansion for all humanity.

On a civilisation level the 22nd. Century brings a new kind of man - a much more caring, loving, idealistic, tactful, congenial, nurturing, intuitive, spiritual, healing and sensitive man but one who is still practical, efficient and rational. A perfect balancing of the masculine and feminine energies. Perhaps the emergence of our S. N. A. G. S. (Sensitive, new age guys) is an indication of the changes already in progress.

Men must empower themselves with new ideas, attitudes and philosophies through the ability to expand the mind to encompass greater dimensions of awareness. To discover who they really are as individuals will give them the opportunities to develop their special talents, skills and themselves - their inner self. This is self-awareness. Certainly not through egotism, manipulation, selfishness, aggression or superiority.

"Head of the house! Boss! Men are superior! Master! Lord!" These classifications belong to a Patriarchal society. This is not self-awareness and it is not *individualisation*! This type of mentality is one of the reasons why there is so much hostility, aggression, hate, war, murder and rape in the world today. Change our consciousness and we can change the World! There will always be differences and these should be recognised but not discriminated against. To share, to educate and to communicate is to enlighten!

> *"There is no hope in a world of hatred:*
> *Only love can produce love."*

Commitment is responsibility. If we have children we are compassionately committed to those children until they can take responsibility for themselves. This means the role we take on is one in which we should enlighten, educate and encourage. Parenting is a compassionate role which must be shared by men as well as women. The younger generation are already accepting these new roles much easier than their older counterparts. Many young women are already changing and therefore man's consciousness is changing also. I see young men change, feed, bath, bottle feed babies and toddlers and do household chores which once was considered 'women's work'. True equality will bring tremendous progress, happiness and understanding for all.

Motherhood is the noblest institution there is! This is not a commitment which should be taken lightly as it is as important as any other career can be. Therefore we have to re-establish, change and rethink our whole perception of this extremely important and special role but again we do not have to become enslaved by it. Remember women have the ability to empower the young and to mould the society of tomorrow through love, truth and light. The consciousness of humanity will eventually expand to encompass new ideals and philosophies which will bring greater awareness for all Karmic and evolutionary growth.

"Each new birth is a chance for enlightenment,
Therefore motherhood is noble."

Mothers should always have blue in their aura as this denotes the ability to teach. The throat chakra is blue - words of wisdom, harmony, peace, tranquillity and spiritual love. This is the role of mothers! There are many mothers who lack this colour in their Auras and therefore their children are lacking as well. Nurture peace, contentment, harmony and love and you will provide the right atmosphere for your children.

There are many who confuse the colour rose pink for great love. Pink is love but it is the love which is associated with the purity of innocence, like that of a child. But also remember children are immature so pink also denotes immaturity. One teacher of Chakras was actually instructing her students the throat chakra had changed (because of the new age) to pink. This is of course not possible. The Chakra belongs to another dimension - and as such is governed by the laws of the universe and the laws of the universe do not change! Just imagine if our throat chakra was pink! We would remain immature in speech and never utter words of wisdom. For those who never grow up this may be possible but for the majority, experience and growth provides Karmic and evolutionary development and wisdom.

There is quite a lot of misconceptions about the colour black. When wearing this colour it actually prevents outside energies from affecting our psyche so therefore wearing black would benefit those who are predisposed to picking up outside negative influences and would be a great benefit to those who meditate in group situations as well as those who counsel others.

> *"Our mind should plan the way*
> *but love direct our steps."*

When we make any commitment to any partnership, marriage included, we must take on responsibility and accountability. This does not mean we have to give ourselves in useless self-sacrifice or martyrdom. Give and take. Use your own discrimination to know if the commitment is not working for the benefit of both parties *through love*. Do not allow dependency, guilt, need or fear to enslave you as this is very easy to do! Once you have learnt to let go and set yourself free you have created the opportunity for growth and for expanding consciousness.

I am continually amazed by the fact that all professional jobs have training programs and University degrees available - yet the positions which require the most responsibility of all, the role of husbands, wives, mothers and fathers do not require any professional training what so ever.

There should be classes available in our society for these extremely important roles and commitments in life. It should not be a hit and miss affair! These are the positions which develop the adults of tomorrow. Happy wives and husbands make happy parents and happy parents make happy children. These classes should be part of the education system and start when children are about twelve years old. At this age they would digest the information and it would become a natural part of their physical, emotional, mental and spiritual development and would help bring equality to all.

Humanitarian Love -	*"Evil destroys! It opposes even other evil. When evil conquers good - evil dies. Good nourishes itself and will grow again, so there is always hope."*

Humanitarian love is the love for all humanity. Divine compassion - the belief in the unity of humankind. It is kindness, empathy, *responsibility and service to others*. Not just limited charity but the ability to give to others from the very core of who you are. The ability to give more of yourself than what is perhaps required - not because of your profession or job but because of your humanitarian spirit - your inner soul energies. Not giving in useless self-sacrifice or martyrdom but to uplift, teach, inspire, motivate and educate. The ability to let your light shine, warming hearts which are sick or just empty of hope and purpose.

Why are there so many displaced sick and starving men, women and children in the world today? Many of those who are born to very poor countries and then die are those who are experiencing their very first lives. Through reincarnation they have the ability for progress. Karma will give them the opportunity eventually to reach a higher level of attainment.

We must remember we are being tested also. How much do *we* do to help them exist? World Vision, Red Cross and many other societies are organisations which are there to enable us to do our share, to help and uplift humanity either at home or abroad. Sometimes in the past when we have given to charities the money has been misused in fraudulent ways. This should never stop anyone from caring and helping others!

Positive Karma is always created through the ability to give unconditionally from the heart, the ability to give openly and generously! Just the act of sharing, caring and giving through divine compassion and unconditional love creates positive energy. This is the true meaning of *Love!*

The word *Love* - Numerologically speaking, vibrates to the 18/9. This vibration gives the ability to bring the body, mind and higher mind together into one cohesive unit so as not to become enslaved by the emotions. 9 is love and healing for *All humankind!* To transcend the needs of personal self through the act of giving. This is Universal love.

It's 'soul' is 11/2 - visionary, freedom, spiritual and upliftment. The ability to tame the animal nature for its ultimate achievement - to accept responsibility for the upliftment of humanity. Love has an 'outer personality' of 7 which is inner reality! Conquest on the mental plane, the bridge between the mental and spiritual realms.

This means we must *think* - be rational - not just feel.

This creates balance - love used through a more rational perspective and not just through the emotions. Love with divine compassion and non-attachment is *pure love!* Then used for the good of all humankind. There is certainly no limitation and bondage here but negatively it can be illusion and delusion gone mad!

The Age of Aquarius is almost upon us:
The age of truth and knowledge.
The age of humanitarian love.

The elections in South Africa in 1994 have united the country. There will be a lot of co-operation still needed to overcome the mental and restless energy which comes from such a giant step in the evolution of humankind. The symbol of Aquarius is the water bearer. She is pouring what seems to be water out of the vessel she is holding. What she is actually doing is pouring *love* onto humanity. (The water symbolises love). It is this love which will eventually unite all humankind.

"Hate does not conquer love. Love conquers hate."

Eventually this will create one race of people and one religion. The 1990's is a time when old traditions, organisations and structures will fall to make way for the new - through a greater humanitarian democracy. Many of these institutions have started to crumble all ready. This is also a time when hidden truth will be uncovered and revealed.

Just some of the structures which have to fall to be reconstructed in the future through more positive environmental and humanitarian concepts are education; private enterprise; money corporations and establishments; religion; health institutions; energy and power structures; Government organisations and the legal system.

Just recently in Sydney - Australia, two Judges were accused of making these biased statements. "When a woman says no - she means yes." The second case: A woman was beaten unconscious then raped. The judge handed down a lesser sentence because in his opinion she wasn't as traumatised as if she had been conscious.

This is not equality!

The legal system seems to fail the very people it is there to defend - the innocent! The economic system has certainly had some major problems and will have more as we head towards the end of the century. In fact the whole economic system is predicted to fall and when it does eventually rise again it will be reconstructed through greater humanitarian ideals and not through greed, dishonesty, manipulation and power.Clinical psychology will be replaced by Karmic psychology for the rehabilitation of the damaged psyche.

The Church has definitely had it's foundations rocked with the many cases of exposed priests who have misused their positions of trust and faith to gratify their own perverted sexual needs and desires. All religions will eventually fall to make way for truth and one universal belief system. We are now seeing all around us the collapse of many of these traditions and institutions. This intiates opportunity for change and positive change creates progress for all.

This glorious age - the age of equality - unification through love is the *Golden age* and will last for approximately 2000 years. But first we must have an ending before we can have a new beginning. So when things seem to be at their lowest ebb have faith, hope, love and understanding for yourself and for others. I feel this quote is quite appropriate for these approaching traumatic times.

"Due to unforeseen circumstances, the light at the end of the tunnel has just gone out..."

and I say to you, " We all have our own light to guide us through times of turmoil. The light of our spirit - strength of spirit."

Many, many, men will not be able to comprehend these changing times, when nothing is permanent, when heartaches and loss multiply and money, work and business structures vanish. Simply because they see most things from a purely logical view point and are not prepared spiritually, emotionally or mentally. This will definitely apply to women also who fear, need, hang on and have not nurtured strength of spirit in times of conflict. Hopefully there will be many women who will empower themselves. If they do - they will become strong, courageous and bring hope, love and upliftment to many through the healing, nurturing, understanding and loving qualities which they possess.

Through those men and women who have prepared themselves physically, emotionally, mentally and spiritually others will gain strength and inspiration to overcome the many problems, heartaches, losses, chaos and havoc that will very soon overtake humankind. This is indeed needed to prepare the way to create a receptive world for our new age - The Golden Age.

Through the heartaches, loss and chaos humanity will surrender to change. Many will unlock the doors of the mind to receive new knowledge, truth and greater understanding. It is only when we are brought to our knees - do we listen! Humanity has become complacent - and the world - a Sodom and Gomorrah.

(Sodom and Gomorrah were the Biblical cities which created destruction through the misuse of their baser physical energies. Sexual perversion ran completely rife there and this in itself over a period of time decreed it's fate. Karma is the law of cause and effect and is the law of the Universe!)

"Strength and gentleness go together."

Expand the mind, understand things have to end for a new beginning and for a change in mass consciousness. Have faith, hope and love and do not look to the self - but look to what you can do for those who have a greater need than you. We must all look to the humanitarian within us and then give to others through love and divine compassion. This is wisdom and a necessary element in crossing the barrier to the light of expanded consciousness. Now is definitely the time for perfecting our natural, creative and healing talents and abilities through the many courses which are available.

"Strive to gain what has not yet been gained.
What has been gained, carefully protect.
Increase what has been protected, by proper means.
What has been increased, bestow upon worthy persons.
These four methods must be applied unfailingly
for the enhancement of humanity."

"The Way of Kings."
Ancient Wisdom from the Sanskrit Vedas.
Translated by Drew Lawrence.

CHAPTER 5

SEX.........   *"Judge a man, not by the work he does,*

   but watch his pleasures!"

So many men and women use - misuse their power for sex. This energy comes from the base chakra. Through just sex one is only expelling energy. What happens then if one uses this sexual energy through love? This opens up other chakras and as one progresses off the purely physical and emotional levels more expansion takes place. Sex used with real love and spiritual truths can actually bring higher expanded consciousness. This means a much healthier and happier outlook for humanity. No prejudices or rigid thinking here! But we must also know sex should only be used with love and commitment and with the right moral intentions and responsibilities.

Throughout history sex has been preached against and called the original sin. It has been the perpetrator of fear, guilt and manipulation. In Greek Mythology, Dionysus the God of wine, joviality and sexual orgies used his power to entice many women to join his orgiastic cult.. He later became an underworld divinity. Aphrodite was also associated with erotic love and seduction. In one of her manifestations she became the Goddess of prostitution which was practiced in her temples. Sexual crimes have been committed throughout time. Even today there are those who murder and rape through aggressive and obsessive passion. For some promiscuity and perverted sexual practises are the custom just for pure physical gratification and indulgence. Religion has created fanatics who have used torture and cruelty to appease their sexual appetites. For others sex has created neurosis, frigidity, hate and repression.

In other words, sex can 'screw' your whole life - if you allow it to!

Perhaps it is the foundation of all disease (dis-ease) but again this has only come about through rigid thought patterns, the misuse and abuse of sexual energy, religious dogma, patterning and conditioning from past and present incarnations and no doubt will again be carried forward into future lifetimes if the conditioning and thought patterns are not changed! There are so many *hang ups* about sex! In the past it was never spoken about and now we use it for everything. Even advertising agencies exlpoit it to promote and sell their clients products! Take heart, time and education will eventually change negative patterning and conditioning, belief systems, needs and desires.

Throughout the ages the many depraved priests who were involved in immoral sexual conduct thought they would change the laws of morality and decency. They decided through their writing of spiritual texts they could make women subservient and the perpetrators of sin - and all children were born in sin. These books were edited and re-edited until they were eventually completed, making sure the material they contained enhanced the 'power of the church.' Over many centuries the very people who were chosen to enlighten and develop humanity have in fact plunged humanity into darkness.

Numerologically speaking: *sex* vibrates to the 12/3 and means joy, expansion, self-expression, light, acceptance and love. It is reversal of thought for a higher spiritual awakening. It will certainly bring loss and heartaches if abused and misused and create negative Karma. Negatively it is extravagance, deceit, loss, indulgence, frivolity, lust, depression and complacency. The Tarot symbolism is the "Hanging Man" - reversal of thought for expanded consciousness and freedom.

Humanity must reverse it's way of thinking about sex as it must not be used and abused or surrounded with fear and guilt. For many this is exactly what sex creates in their lives - The Hanging Man - through rigid thought patterns, belief systems and through the misuse and abuse of this energy.

> ***"There are no flames like passion and hate.***
> ***Desire, is a raging torrent and illusion, is the net."***

Humankind must direct sexual energy to a higher positive use. This is one of the reasons why women must empower themselves positively. Sex must *not* be used as a commodity to be bartered, ransomed, bought or sold. It is not dirty! It should not be a duty! It should not be a chore. On the other hand many give themselves freely in sexual activity simply because they think *love* is the prize! This is an illusion! We must all understand sex is an act *of love*. A beautiful, expansive, joyous, expression to be mutually shared in the act of love. It is exciting, rejuvenating and transcendental. It is not our 'animal nature' gone rampant and should never be used indiscriminately.

We are here to transform negative energies and to regenerate ourselves to a higher consciousness. This means the right laws of morality and integrity must be adhered to. You do not sell your soul for sex! If humanity uses sex without the right moral codes, laws and wrong sexual practices over a long period of time it creates a Sodom and Gomorrah and will eventually bring down the civilisation. The pathway to freedom - liberation does not mean the freedom to practice free sex. It means to use integrity, discrimination, responsibility, morality and the right aspirations on the journey to the light.

"Sex should never become a focus,
it should always be used with love."

A client wanted spiritual direction. When he came to me for his Numerology chart, I could see in his last lifetime he allowed his physical and emotional energies to limit and bind him. His propensity for higher spiritual growth and expansion will not be possible if he continues with the same patterns he created last life. With difficulty he is learning to negate his need for sexual conquests - but still feels his lust for sexual pleasure. His almost desperate *need* for a relationship masks this part of his nature. Last lifetime he was a monk in Asia and he negated his higher spiritual unfoldment for emotional and physical gratification.

This lifetime he has the ability to expand upon his spirituality and not come from any rigid, biased or indulgent ideals of past lives. To use the mind positively! To think! To be rational, to control and then to go within and rest on the spirit through solitude and meditation. If we are to become aware of who we are and where we are going then it is vital we become responsible for our own actions, physically, emotionally, mentally and spiritually. How? Through discipline and control not only achieved through strength but through positive perceptivity.

This is wisdom! To understand true spirituality does not necessarily mean we have to deny ourselves true love or to condemn ourselves to guilt when we express that love through sex. Spirituality of course does *not* mean we fill our lives with continual rounds of sexual encounters and immerse ourselves in a life of promiscuity. Higher spiritual expansion always demands discipline and responsibility.

When we give ourselves into bondage through our needs and desires, we imprison ourselves to feelings and to baser reality. To help him transcend his lust for sexual pleasure, he should *think* first . Learn to control and discipline his thought processes - to use the mind through positive means!

I also suggested if possible he should find a partner who shares his spiritual views and together they should learn the art of tantric sex. This way he would learn to control his sexual urges through positive means. He would then be in a position to raise sexual energy to a higher power - for transcendental power and not just for the sexual gratification of his baser physical needs and desires. His spiritual unfoldment depends on it!

Husbands and wives would benefit from the use of tantric sex in their lives. It would teach many women to transcend the mental blockages which have been created from past or present life sexual experiences and men would learn to transcend the purely physical and selfish connation of the sexual act. Tantric sex is a means to develop sexual practice to a higher spiritual level if used with truth, love, morality and integrity.

The word Tantric comes from the ancient Hindi writings connected to the belief of Shakti - the feminine principle. The purpose of tantras is to establish philosophies and disciplines in our lives through the correct and proper use of energy, including sexual energy. Why? To obtain liberation from ignorance and the end of continual life, death and rebirth. Sex has been shrouded in ignorance over many lifetimes. Pure ignorance as well as the ignorance of baser needs and desires!

Sex alone is not love!

It is an expression of love. Love needs to be expressed in many ways and one of these is through the sexual act. Through the love we feel we can then experience supreme ecstasy and this then gives us the ability to uplift and expand the consciousness through it's transcendental power. It is not evil! It should not be lust! It is not a common utility to be explored and used in manipulative power games or just for releasing emotional frustration. *It is pure love* transcended to its' highest expression through the vehicle of sexual energy. It is natural and it must be used through the purity of true love, commitment and *spiritual power* to bring an expanded consciousness.

When men and women realise this they will find themselves more balanced and tuned into harmony, sharing and caring. Loving relationships will bring much joy, fulfilment, happiness and insight. They say "Love makes the world go round." Today they seem to be using sex and not love. This will always bring chaos - A Sodom and Gomorrah! (AIDS is a perfect example)

Through the positive use of these energies women can empower themselves and this in turn will bring progress and tremendous change to male consciousness. This is indeed a woman's power! However she must know how to use this power for the benefit and good of all. Certainly *not* through emotional dependency and need or manipulative power games but through *the power of love.* We will always reap what we sow, from one lifetime to the next. This is Karma!

> ***"Let, not many of you, become teachers,***
> ***my brethren, for you know, that we who teach,***
> ***shall be judged with greater strictness."***

Many so called spiritual leaders, healers, teachers, advisers, guides and writers misuse their positions of authority and trust to manipulate others in sexual games and seem to fall into the trap or net of sexual conquest and promiscuity. Sex should not be a need. It is not something with which to prove one's worth through masculine or feminine power and manipulation.

There are those who try to find their self-esteem through sex. This is not possible! This is a trap of delusion. Self-esteem comes from self! The perception of self! Your perception! Continual sexual encounters will only confuse you more and belongs to the purely physical plane. There is no progress here! This pathway of promiscuity is one of darkness. Growth comes through self-awareness, empowerment and an expanded consciousness as we journey to the light of greater understanding.

The need for sexual conquest is certainly negative patterning and conditioning which must be overcome. These patterns may come from egotism or sometimes through the need to find love for self. This will never come from sex! We can never prove who we are through sexual energy. Humanity must come from a higher consciousness than permissive sensibilities!

Transcend physical need - sexual gratification.

Through the control of the mental plane from physical and emotional desires and fantasies, we can actually transcend this life of *limitation and bondage - of base sexual needs and desires.* Just because we *feel* desire, need and even love we do not have to *use* this energy. However many do through fear! In case of! What if! I can't say no! I need! I might miss out! Perhaps this is love! *Love,* might be the prize! This is only gratification of our baser energies through fear and guilt. If true love is involved - you don't have to barter or sell yourself for sex.

Learning to transcend these *feelings* we have to *think*! We have to *use* our will-power, responsibility, discrimination and control. We do not have to hate ourselves for feelings or live with continual guilt as this is more negative patterning! We just have to be aware we are here to transform and regenerate all the negative conditions in our lives. *This is Wisdom!*

Sexual affairs are only a quick fix! Feelings of need, loneliness, heartache, unfulfilment and the need for excitement require new thoughts, ideals, attitudes and directions. This brings the ability to change, to grow, to evolve and to transcend baser emotional and physical energy. By creating negative behaviour we will perpetuate more negative patterns which will have to be overcome in future lifetimes.

> *"Sound, touch, sight and smell - any one of these senses is capable of causing calamity."*
>
> ....
>
> *"Any one of these senses when uncontrolled can bring misfortune. When all five are unrestrained, destruction is inevitable."*
>
> *"The Way of Kings."*
> *Ancient Wisdom from the Sanskrit Vedas.*
> *Translated by Drew Lawrence.*

We must change our focus from inner reality to outer reality if we are to find new directions, ideas, and philosophies. Off self - off need and off physical gratification!

When we have learned to control and transcend our baser needs and desires to a higher vibration of love consciousness, sex becomes love, - it is joy, it is beauty, it is pleasure, it is pure, it is exciting, it is transcendental it is supreme ecstasy and should always be used with *true love and responsibility.* Through the proper use of sex through purity and love we can actually reach enlightenment but only when one is ready - through the Kundalini Power. To reach this stage one must have corssed those barriers to the higher realms of transcendental spiritual union.

What is Kundalini? Kundalini is our life force - the force of the body! It is only through our Karmic and evolutionary growth this life force starts to uncoil itself and begin it's journey through the chakras. Remember it is only through positive growth these chakras open completely creating beautiful whirlpools of rotating energy until it reaches the sixth. 'The Third Eye' area. Eastern Philosophy maintains until Kundalini has reached the heart centre we have not even begun our journey of awareness. To be completely awakened each centre has specific elements which must be mastered. The heart centre has twelve petals of personality which must be transformed. In very rare cases it reaches the seventh - the thousand petal lotus. This is illumination or enlightenment! Where is Kundalini?

The base of Kundalini Power is situated exactly halfway between the organ of reproduction and the organ of excretion. Through pure love and higher spiritual energies we can eventually raise this power to a elevated position to achieve growth and an expanded consciousness even illumination. Illumination brings knowledge, neutrality and liberation. If we use sex on just the purely base level for need, desire, lust, sensation and gratification of the senses - it degenerates - not regenerates! Again do not mistake need for love. We cannot evolve to a higher consciousness and illumination through this pathway.

Women's sexuality comes from inner reality. Man's sexuality is from outer reality. Through the sexual act man gives to woman. She then uses and transcends this energy for it's ultimate expression of transcendental power for herself and then gives this power back to him. Through purity and true love this can then raise the consciousness of both.

Throughout the New Age women will have the ability to change and regain their power the right way. Not through the need to dominate, control or manipulate but through respect and honour. They will hold the divine secrets within themselves. Not through the needs, desires, bondage, dependencies and manipulation of baser emotional and physical energy! Positive power will only come through the ability to *love* from a higher dimension of awareness. Because of the change in women's consciousness, male consciousness will change as well. This certainly should not be a threat to men, in fact in time it will bring equality and expanded consciousness to both.

This makes the path to the light much easier simply because our perception is not clouded by illusions and deception. Fear comes from not knowing and understanding. Truth and knowledge bring expansion and higher awareness and gives us the ability to find the light. This definitely does not mean women should take on the role of *goddesses.* This is only another misconception and a distortion of the truth. This is as bad as men being *lord and master.* The evolution of humanity is trying to go forwards not backwards. By all means believe in feminine power but do not go to extremes and create more negative conditions which will have to eventually fall to create balance.

These 'cult' practices are geared to ritual and segregation of the sexes. Ritual is a primitive expression for worship and as such, belongs to the past. It is time to expand the intellect and let go of the needless encapsulation of all unnecessary clutter and garbage and set ourselves free. We are all on a journey to the light of expanded consciousness therefore we do not need to take on any more entrapments for negative patterning.

"Desire is a trap.
Lustful desire,
makes pigs of people
and slaves of pigs.
A single word,
makes possible all civilisations;
a small word,
a magic word,
it frees, it transforms.
 You must whisper it to yourself.
The word is No."

PART 2

EXPANDING CONSCIOUSNESS

CHAPTER 6

HAPPINESS......... *"Defeat can be turned into victory,*

if you first change your mind,

then change your need."

Needs and desires create restlessness, heartaches, unfulfilment and unhappiness. Centralisation - centring on the self creates imprisonment. This is definitely negative ego energy and this in turn brings judgment. We will never be happy when we judge others and worst of all we will never be free. We are all on a journey to freedom therefore it is imperative we let judgment go! Happiness and joy are the two most important ingredients for higher spiritual unfoldment. These come from acceptance! Acceptance not only of others but of ourselves. When we learn not to judge but to accept we can let go of all the undesirable actualities from our lives.

Judging and criticising others prevents us from seeing the truth. Our perception and our vision become clouded and then illusion and delusion becomes the reality. This prevents us from moving forward for growth and expansion. When this happens, true happiness cannot and will not be experienced. The more we care for the happiness and well being of others the more we will experience happiness and joy for ourselves.

An Ancient Eastern Philosophy

"Winners sow hatred because the loser must suffer,
Give up winning and losing and find joy.
Losers can gain by changing direction - tranquillity!

Acceptance is the foundation for happiness and love. Acceptance gives us the ability to love self. *Then we must develop faith!* 'Faith can move mountains - that is faith in ourselves.' With faith and will-power - civilisations are built, new structures, ideals and ideas are created.

Do not be too hard in your own criticisms and try not to seek perfection within yourself or others. Nurture individualisation and self-empowerment! Learn to laugh because *laughter is the elixir of life.* Remember to always create beauty, light, love and faith in your everyday existence. Take care of the little things which bring feelings of pleasure to the spirit. You don't have to become frivolous, indulgent or extravagant, just a gentle pampering of self - loving self. Through the ability to expand consciousness we create an abundance of joy and happiness.

To transcend all physical encapsulation for neutrality, liberation and enlightenment we must first expand our thought processes. To do this we very often have to reverse our ideals, our attitudes and our belief systems. This enables us to let go of our stumbling blocks and all the needs and desires which limit and bind. Judgment is always a major barrier which must be overcome for growth, expanded consciousness and freedom. If we are so busy looking at something someone else has done how can we look at ourselves? Judgment may just be an excuse for not looking at self! It brings negative perceptions and the inability to move forward. How can we ever find faith and happiness when we *hang on* to these negative energies?

Judgment prevents us from seeing who we are and in many instances blocks the pathway of others. When we take on the role of judment we restrict, limit and bind. This is the stage of *tunnel vision* because we are unable to expand our thought processes to the higher realms of consciousness. No wonder we lose the plot!

"Judge not a man lest thou be judged."

Through the simple act of judging others we more often than not fail ourselves. We set up patterns and conditions which must be eventually be broken because of all the negative repercussions which emanate from judgement.

Let go set yourself free and find all the happiness and joy which comes from expanding your own awareness. Judgment is egotism - centralisation - centering on the self. Inner reality through insecurity and lack of self-empowerment. Women must be extremely careful not to let gossip and frivolity become a pattern in their lives. Gossip can very often lead to judgment. Gossip and frivolity are just two of the negative energies the word, *woman* vibrates to. (These are the negative energies of 3).

An Ancient Buddhist Philosophy

"No failure is forever. There is always change and new beginnings. We are born again and yet again."

Complete trust in the higher scheme of things especially the Universal Laws is the catalyst for faith, hope and happiness. Happiness is what helps us transcend the physical world of 'heartache and pain.' More so when we understand these are the very energies which become the creative course for our transformation to the higher realms of spiritual reality. Life on earth is very transient and eventually we all have to die! We cannot just disappear to the heavenly fields, body and all whenever we wish. It is impossible to enter heaven in a physical form! We can only enter through the spirit realm therefore we have to discard our body eventually. In other words we have to let go of physical life. So it stands to reason if we are ever to find happiness in life we must also be able to find happiness in death!

Death is as inevitable as night and day. Fear and superstition surround this final transition which eventually comes to all of us. We seem to want to stay in our earthly body forever but as age creeps upon us we tend to change our minds and welcome death as a respite from the ravages of time. This always brings to mind the feelings I have had with birth. As with death, giving birth is not always an easy process and we do not always look to the actual birth with love. However as the nine months come to an end we welcome the time with great anticipation and joy. Not only because of our wonderful new born baby but because we have reached a stage of fatigue, discomfort and frustration. Nature has a wonderful way of creating the perfect timing.

What is death? It is the transition to the *other side* or as some prefer to call it, to heaven. It is an ending! It is the ending of one identity for another one to eventually take over. Through the many lives we experience we will eventually have the ability to transform and to transcend all earthly encumbrances. This is why *hanging on* to anything and anyone on the earth plane creates limitation and bondage.

This continual death and rebirth cycle will help us to ultimately penetrate these illusions and to understand how transient earth life really is. The thought of death very often brings sorrow and fear. For some it may even create guilt and remorse. Through the use of any obsessive emotional energy we create the inability to function in a normal or rational manner. The pain we feel is normally for ourselves and not for the loved ones who have departed. Do not shed tears for those who have escaped the confines of earthly encumbrances for awhile because they are the ones who have gone *home*. Death is an ending for a new beginning! The gestation period of nine months is again the end of one existence for a new one to begin.

An old Egyptian philosophy:

"Nor does sorrowful weeping,
save anyone from the grave."

Death is really our Karmic reward. It gives us the ability to try again and again on our journey to freedom. To overcome to become! To let go of the world of attachments and the misconceptions of physical reality to find the truth. Through faith, wisdom and love we will learn to accept our path with happiness and joy simply because this is the path to complete autonomy and freedom. The path which eventually leads us to the light of a higher consciousness - to the immortality of our spirit - to the end of our rounds of death and rebirth to the earth plane.

To understand the meaning of life we have to understand the meaning of death. Death is the transition into light. *'The Radiance of Pure Reality.'* It is going *home* to our temporary home. If we loved the thought of death we would find it too easy to end *life* and suicide would come naturally. Of course this is wrong! We have chosen a life to learn something so learn we must. Therefore we must all use 'life' as a creative course for learning. We simply cannot end it when it becomes too difficult.   If we decide to take the easy way out and end it then we would have to return and repeat it all again. What an atrocious thought! This could be the very life which offers us the ability to progress through a more contemplative and profound perception. Therefore we must learn to accept responsibility for all our choices - our decisions, especially *our life.* This is why we chose it in the first place - to learn - to evolve and to transcend!

"Time can change everything,
if you can wait for just awhile.
Into your life it will bring
happiness, love and everything."

Time does change everything. Everything we are has taken many lifetimes to achieve. Awareness takes time to develop. Death gives us the ability to try again and again, to overcome to become. Therefore each and every lifetime we should be able to get closer to freedom and to the immortality of our spirit. We should not fear death - there is nothing to fear but fear itself! Knowing, understanding and accepting this brings higher consciousness and the ability to see death is only the vehicle we board to *go home.*

Death then is only a means to enter another dimension of existence and should bring great joy and happiness instead of sadness and misery. If we fear death we reject the whole meaning of life. Death brings to all of us the ability to try again. Another existence - another life - to wipe the slate clean. To transcend all misery and heartaches and find immortality of the spirit from the encapsulation of physical reality.

> *"Happiness brings life to death,*
> *It brings light to life.*
> *It gives warmth, hope and faith,*
> *It is sunshine, it is spring, it is energy,*
> *it is love and it is*
> *acceptance of life and living."*
> RE *Magnets of the Universe*

Happiness lifts the spirit and it eases the pressures of life. Happiness regenerates and uplifts not only ourselves but others. Happiness creates and makes all things possible. It is one of the great miracles of life.

> *"Time moves not like a river, from here to there:*
> *we do that. Time moves in waves: it ebbs and flows.*
> *There is a time for everything."*

A numerology client had experienced a past life regression prior to visiting me. She had found in her last life she had belonged to the religious sect, The Quakers. When I looked at her "Karmic Growth Of The Soul," (Re - Magnets Of The Universe) which was the 3, I could see she was back again to expand her vision. To learn acceptance and to change her rigid belief systems. Through acceptance she would learn to expand the mind to a much higher consciousness and to also use her creativity with inspiration, vision and tolerance.

This life she had chosen to reverse the rigid thought patterns of her previous incarnation and to experience joy and happiness in life and living. To understand acceptance and expansion would enable her to transform her past rigid ideas of spirituality into a higher dimension of love, truth and faith. Even her experiences in life were chosen to expand on this philosophy. Her marriage ended when her husband left her for another man! She now counsels those men and women who have shared these same experiences.

So you see we must all learn to extend our vision - not to judge others or to become rigid and dogmatic in our belief systems or ourselves. To enjoy life - to experience happiness, faith, optimism and love - to expand upon and share with others our wisdom and creativity. It is extremely important to experience optimism and faith in life and living and to know that happiness and joy are absolutely necessary for expanding consciousness.

You have to lighten up, laugh, be happy, have faith and learn acceptance. Optimism, happiness and faith will create hope and hope creates the ability to function positively on all levels of existence. When humanity loses hope the light goes out. This light is the light of the spirit!

Happiness, joy and laughter are the essential ingredients for maintaining this light in our lives. It takes more muscles to frown than to laugh - so why isn't there more laughter? It washes away the darkness of our lives and puts a whole new perspective on life and living. When all is said and done this is not all that there is to our existence - we are here to learn, to grow, to evolve and to transform all our negative energies on our journey to the light.

"Master yourself, because it is fun."

The Medical world says we stimulate the endorphines within the body when we laugh - these are called the happy hormones. These help the heart, the lungs and all the body to function positively. Laughter alleviates pain and rigidity - it relaxes - it releases. So it stands to reason it is good for you. To become too focused on our problems brings limitation and bondage. We cannot create expansion of the mind through focusing on just ourselves. If we do we very often become fixed, rigid and centralised. The I, Me and My philosophy!

Look out to the external world - expand the vision, find positive points in people - not the negative. If you can't, then let them go completely. Do not concern yourself with the negativity of others. Even change directions if need be. There are always those who will never change in this lifetime. That is their problem and their Karmic lesson. Your concern this lifetime is your own transformation and regeneration. Many times we hang onto judgment because we feel denied. This is negative ego energy - love yourself - empower yourself - nurture yourself. When we transcend self we expand our awareness.

Therefore true self-awareness and expanded consciousness cannot come from judging others. Are we victims - or do we victimise ourselves - by not loving and respecting self or for hanging onto the many negative energies which we create in our lives and even in the lives of those we love? Find your inner light through the expansion into the higher realms of consciousness through meditation and esoteric knowledge. This will always bring a broader perspective on the true realities of our existence. Allow all negative situations in your life to become the catalyst for growth. Seek *and you will find!* Faith in life is the acceptance in the higher scheme of things. Spread joy and sunshine not only into your own life but into the lives of others through hope, love, faith and optimism. Fill your life not just with white light but with golden light!

Happiness comes from the expansion of the mind and the spirit, our own divine spirit. To expand the mind and spirit we first have to let go of all the energies which limit and bind us - and find neutrality. Once we have liberated ourselves from all repression, true happiness and joy will come from within. It is a state of mind! There are those who continually strive to find something or someone outside themselves to make them happy. This is the need for attachment! This is almost impossible! Happiness comes from inner reality, it comes from the spirit! It is truth, faith, acceptance, hope and happiness which eventually sets us free.

It is pure pleasure just to be happy. To be free is to be happy. To be free is to transcend all physical manifestations and heartaches - to even accept them then rise above them. To feel tremendous joy and happiness *in being who you are.* To know within you lies a faith in higher consciousness which defies the pain and suffering of the earth plane. This happiness brings beauty, light, love and faith into our lives - into our very own fundamental existence.

> ***"All the days of the oppressed are wretched,***
> ***but the cheerful heart has a continual feast."***

Strip away the face of darkness and despair. Happiness exists! It is in the trees, the birds, the flowers, in all of nature, in giving, in humanity and in yourself. It is seeing, understanding and using higher truths to lighten the way! It is a part of accepting the who and what you are. To understand expansion and freedom comes from a higher realm of cognisance. This, then gives you the ability to love and accept yourself and then to love and accept others.

Self-awareness brings the ability to understand our inner self - our psyche. Through developing this inner reality we tap into the reservoir of hidden talents of many lifetimes. We are all here to achieve something! There are hidden talents and abilities within each of us which can and should be brought out into the conscious world of thought and action. We are what we think! We must create what we want to be! This is not all that there is to your evolutionary soul growth. There are many other dimensions to your personality which have brought you to this present incarnation. Tap your hidden power - expand the soul consciousness. *Seek and you will find!* Believe in your power - expand your vision to encompass the whole spectrum of the *'who and what you are.'* You have been a long time upon the way.

"The way is a journey as long as life itself."

Have you ever wondered why you love something with great passion? It might be music, dancing, perhaps singing, art, pottery, writing, teaching, healing, astrology or even numerology. Have you ever wanted to do something so much but felt it required too much effort?

We all bring back past patterning and conditioning from our previous lifetimes. These longings may not be as crazy as they sound. Do not deny yourself the ability to try to find and develop your own creative potential. These are divine gifts which you may have earnt over many lifetimes. Senility comes to many who have let go of their creative purpose. Creativity gives us the need to create - to motivate and this keeps us busy. When we give up - we die!

"Pick yourself up, brush yourself down,
and start all over again."

The mind is the power house of operations! It is like a computer! Feed it negative thoughts and garbage and this is what you will receive to live your life by. Feed it positive thoughts and love and this is what you will become. When life stands still and there is no direction change your focus and learn something! Do courses even if you have to borrow books. You may decide to give some of your time to helping others through the many organisations which are available. Or you may just want to create and transform your house or garden into something beautiful. Learn meditation! Penetrate the illusions of physical reality and find a greater dimension to your existence. Higher spiritual development demands that we go beyond the world of objectivity to one of subjectivity! (intangible) Develop your spiritual growth through solitude and if you can astral travel!

Through the ability to change focus through positive action, life becomes brighter, clearer and our vision expands into new dimensions. This in turn creates a better quality of life for ourselves and for others. Whatever we study and learn we have the ability to bring back as inner knowledge to help us develop further in our future lifetimes. Knowledge and creativity are never wasted no matter at what age we start.

Through the *expansion* of our inner creativity, intellectual skills and spiritual philosophies we can change negative energies into positive ones and this in turn brings inspirational thoughts for greater creative reality. All *expansion* therefore brings the ability for many changes in our lives and is the catalyst for personal growth - physically, emotionally, mentally and spiritually! Greater unfoldment in one's evolutionary development always creates a change in consciousness and this in turn brings a tremendous sense of freedom, happiness and joy.

Through creativity - the ability to create we are able to build civilisations and to build ourselves. This creates beauty, love, harmony and balance in our lives. Eventually our consciousness expands to question the who and what we are and the very meaning of life. It is through destruction and negativity we plunge ourselves and others into darkness!

"Happiness then is expressing joy in life and living. It accepts, it creates, it loves, it beautifies and it lights the way for others. It transcends the obstacles and trials of life with optimism and faith. Happiness never loses hope - it is eternal, it is the spring of miracles, it is the fountain of youth, it is the rainbow of life, it is the sun, the moon, the stars and it is freedom."

"If the rain of compassion
falls on the dominion of hell
and the light of wisdom
shines on it, then faith takes root
and blossoms of joy
will spread their fragrance
and it becomes pure land:
If one's mind is pure,
all one's surroundings
are pure also.

CHAPTER 7

WILL-POWER....   *"If the world seems unfair to fatalists,*

it is because they come to believe that

they cannot change or improve.

If there is fate, it is fated that we

make our own lives."

Will-power - power of the will! This is an extremely important step in our evolutionary development. Without will-power all achievement is impossible! To change, to learn, to progress, to work, to overcome, to strive, to achieve, to transform, to regenerate, to evolve and to transcend;

No will-power - no action - no growth.

A perfect example of this on a civilisation level is the following: Some 5,000 years ago a civilisation flourished in the Indus Valley. It was a magnificent, progressive, prosperous and beautiful culture. There were sewage systems, tiled bathrooms with running hot and cold water and even drainage systems. What happened?

This civilisation found the truth - the truth about reincarnation! Through the misappropriation of this belief they presumed they didn't have to try any more! They did not have to use the power of the will, their own will-power for achievement. They felt that now they could put everything off until the next lifetime, then the next and even the next. After all they thought Karma is choice anyway - it is free will.

Over many lifetimes if this becomes the mentality and reality for a whole civilisation with a population of thousands, the civilisation goes backwards. Individually the same thing will happen. Remember *karma* is cause and effect. If we do not *use* the power of the will we will never create or achieve anything. There would never be any evolutionary growth or development.

This requires discipline, control, strength and courage. Karmicly this lesson comes to many. Some of the individuals who become priests or who choose a monastic life choose so because of the discipline which may be needed to overcome previous negative patterning. Discipline, strength and courage creates the use of our own conscious will.

Many individuals continually go to classes, lectures and seminars looking for the answers to their problems hoping to find some quick fix. Unless these people use *their own will-power* they will not change. Truth and knowledge is not wisdom! Wisdom comes from *using* truth and knowledge with divine compassion in our lives for all positive achievement. Everything comes back to the self. When someone finds success it is because they have used their conscious will to become self-empowered on this level of existence.

"The future is a dream, never realised:
The past is a phantom. Now is the only reality.
You need all of yourself to live it."

There are those who believe attainment and making money is not spiritual. *This is not necessarily so!* This is just another level which many have to master, another lesson of self-empowerment mandatory for the evolutionary growth of humanity. We all live on the physical plane and as such have to exist. It is the *love of money and greed* which is wrong. To attain and accumulate just for self - for completely selfish reasons. Just look at the word 'selfish.' It is made from the word 'self.' Concentrating on just the self is *egotism*. There are many spiritual people who have chosen to become empowered on the material level through the creation of tangible reality for the implementation of their Karmic and evolutionary lessons.

Motivation is essential for achievement and brings with it the ability to create. Creativity brings with it initiative, inspiration, imagination, inception, construction and invention.

The power of the conscious will creates self-empowerment! Empowerment of self creates motivation and motivation creates action. Without action we all too often negate our evolutionary and Karmic growth not just in one lifetime but many. Do you realise we always fear what we need to learn? There are those who will always hide behind distorted perceptions of right and wrong. This is why Karmic obligations are so difficult. If they were easy they wouldn't be lessons. Some are harder than others because we reap what we sow. Once we become aware and understand the reasons for being here - the very meaning of life itself - then the path becomes easier.

To change our perception creates the catalyst for growth. Through the ability to change we cease to come from ignorance, deception and fantasy. Truth and knowledge must always be used the right way to achieve wisdom. The highest attainment for all of us is the balancing of our own life's forces. To achieve mastery over self. Self-empowerment!

There are many individuals who visit clairvoyants time after time for emotional direction. It is very easy to put our lives on hold and forget our true purpose is to empower self through strength, courage, discipline and individualisation. How many of us keep waiting for someone else to come into our life to change it? Waiting for that special person to make us happy, successful and fulfilled may never happen. This may have to come from our own power our own self-empowerment!

There are times when many have the opportunity to meet that special someone to share their lives with. However this should never take precedence over the journey to freedom, neutrality and liberation. The more empowered we are as individuals the more we can direct our paths to greater spiritual attainments.

Without effort and willpower this will *never* happen. This is the path of least resistance. To actually negate Karmic and evolutionary development because of personal needs, desires and fantasies will prolong our journey to the light. 'To thine own self be true, means - *responsibility to the self*'! This is achieved through unconditional belief in the '*personal self*'.

To believe in self may be extremely difficult but when we develop, understand and accept ourselves we have the ability to grow and to evolve into beautiful, loving and compassionate beings. To reverse our negative traits into positive ones. This means we not only become responsible *to* the self but we become responsible *for* the self - for everything we are and everything we do.

Many individuals who do not believe in themselves unconditionally, lack emotional willpower. This will more often than not have repercussions on the rest of their lives. They may think they have power but in most cases it is not positive willpower. There are those people who use abusive power to manipulate others to do their will. If we cannot empower ourselves through positive means we will confine and chain ourselves to a life of manipulation, uselessness and servitude. A life of limitation and bondage! This in turn brings lack of strength, discipline and responsibility to fulfil all our Karmic and evolutionary obligations from the past, present and future.

> *"To be happy, spiritual and free,*
> *Is my only true reality."*

Judith a Numerology client possesses very powerful numbers! I felt quite strongly she had abused her power in her last life and she was here to work through it again. This time the right way! I was intrigued with what her last life had been? When we met to go through her chart she told me she had been a black witch! (She had a regression into past lives) This explained it all! Some of the same patterns were re-emerging. This life she had come back to find and develop her power the right way. Her destiny suggested she perfect her talents and skills. She had certainly achieved this through the many healing abilities she possessed. Her previous life as a black witch created power and authority but without any true knowledge and wisdom. In her early twenties she had tried prostitution again repeating patterns set up in her last life on the extreme baser level.

Her numbers suggested she must transcend the purely physical plane for higher spiritual understanding. Meditation would provide the means to go within and find the seeds of life and is vital for harmony, insight and peace. To overcome past negative energies of selfishness, greed and manipulation and to journey to the light. She found it hard to empower herself on a positive level. She kept collapsing on her emotions. Her power emerged sometimes in extremely negative and manipulative ways - a repeat of past life conditioning as a black witch. Through the implementation of her work - through the ability to master the will with strength, discipline, discrimination and responsibility she can use her own power - to empower herself. This will enable her to find success through positive achievement! To find a new sense of direction through the ability to transcend all negative patterning and conditioning from the misuse and abuse of power.

Through the need to simply reverse the power of darkness to the power of light or to change consciousness from the power of evil to the power of good we can all 'overcome to become'. When we misuse our power to the detriment of others - we will always reap what we sow. This is why it is so difficult to reverse our negativity to positive thoughts and action. Sometimes we are not even aware of these negative patterns in our lives.

There are many women who use their sexual energies to manipulate men in their quest for position and power. This will always create negative Karma and will have to be sorted out consciously - now - or in future lifetimes to bring the changes needed for positive evolutionary growth.

"The truth about magic is that it is unreal:
That life itself is unreal, Illusions created by our minds."

Will-power builds, it constructs, it changes, it transforms, it regenerates, it explores, it progresses, it expands, it activates, it empowers, it executes, it revives, it energises. Civilisations are built on will-power and action. Personal development and evolutionary growth are not possible without the power of the will - self-empowerment!

> *"One who is slack in his work is brother*
> *to one who destroys."*

This is a time when will-power seems to be missing in a sea of despair and darkness. The familiar patterns and structures are falling and people seem to be lost. For many the will seems to be bent and broken. It is these same individuals who are choosing the negative path - the path of least resistance! If this became the reality for everyone there would never be any growth or development! We must not lose the ability to bounce back after set backs, obstacles, heartaches and pain. We must nurture strength of spirit to transcend and transform the negative conditions in our lives.

There are many young people and even the not so young who want to leave these traumatic times behind and use suicide as the means of escape. We have picked this very life to build and create not only for ourselves but for others. Without strength, courage and discipline we cannot become empowered! The courage to carry on and structure our lives becomes paramount and obviously at times extremely difficult. However by developing strength of spirit through self actualisation, we are eventually able to use our conscious will for positive achievement.

This will always induce a predilection for greater knowledge and understanding on our journey to the light. How many times has worry and fear created restrictions in your life? Strength of spirit is positive energy and creates faith which will always change and revitalise our senses for positive direction.

"The blows of life transform us."

Here is another example to explain the importance of will-power in our lives. (Re "Magnets Of The Universe") Marrianne was extremely loving, vibrant, beautiful, interesting, intelligent and very creative. As a child she was always told how much she was loved and how beautiful she really was. Marrianne was a very loving daughter and sister and at seventeen she made the decision to leave home. When she was eighteen she decided to lose weight!

Within six months she achieved her goal but continued, thus allowing her needs to become obsessional. In her opinion this was the only way she could control her life. These aspects are worse in todays society where the 'perfect body creates the perfect woman' theory is accepted and is the epitome of *illusion and delusion* in our lives! Of course this is not control! It is *out of control* as is all obsessive behaviour. This played havoc on her work, her relationships and her perception with reality. When we live with distorted perceptions we create many undesirable realities in our lives and in the lives of those we love.

Her problem lay deep within as she could not love and accept herself. This was from negative patterning created from previous lifetimes. Even as a child she would say she was not going to live long. (Perhaps a memory of past patterns) She created similar patterning in this life. Her Karmic obligation this lifetime was to break this negative patterning. Definitely not to go to extremes but through the ability to maintain balance in her life and to master her own conscious will. Her Pathway Through Life was the 56/11/2. This is *balance*. Many 56/11/2's become obsessive, unstable and erratic and this then precipitates erratic and unstable conditions not only in their lives but in the lives of others. Her Destiny 8.... To empower herself through positive achievement, with strength, discipline, responsibility and discrimination.

Through courage and the use of her own power of the will she could change, reverse and transform the negative conditioning of previous lifetimes and this lifetime. To overcome she would become! However she could not or would not change her obsessional behaviour! She could not let go of negative patterning. She even said herself, "I wish there was another way," perhaps she meant *an easier way*. At twenty seven years of age she took her own life.

We must break all our negative patterning and conditioning to journey to golden light and to freedom. We must all learn to truly love ourselves, to let go of guilt and hate from the past and present. This then becomes our protection, our safety net to help us grow and transcend the misconceptions of earthly reality.

> *"Our perception of ourselves is the only thing that prevents us from higher achievements. It either makes us or breaks us."*

The fact remains even when we change our negative thought patterns to reverse our way of thinking we will still have to use - *The power of will*. It is only through our own strength, courage and discipline we can overcome, transform and regenerate. Life is a school - if we don't pass our exams we will come back and repeat the same lessons. This change must come through our conscious will - our conscious mind! Truth and knowledge will always bring insight, understanding and awareness but we will still have to use our own will-power to create the transformation which is needed for our evolutionary growth, development and eventual liberation.

"What happens is all our own doing - Karma.
Each life is a lesson: If we kill ourselves,
we must live this life again."

This definitely applies to all obsessive behaviour! Especially, alcohol and drug abuse, as these very often come from past life patterning and conditioning. Alcohol and drugs affect the spirit. When astral travelling if on drugs or alcohol, individuals actually visit the lower base planes and this does not create positive situations for growth. The soul or spirit needs to visit *the heavenly fields* or *home* as often as possible for sustenance.

So if one is continually under the intoxication of drugs and drink there is no renewal or nourishment for the soul as this is not available from the baser astral planes. Ultimately this creates feelings of dejection, deficiency, misconception, fallacy, carelessness, hopelessness and hallucination. This in turn creates the abuse of our physical, emotional, mental and spiritual energies. It may free the spirit from the earthly body but it still limits and binds us to the misconception and fantasies of a baser reality. This pathway degenerates, it does not regenerate!

Marijuana is a mind altering drug. It creates illusion, delusion and escapism. In Mexico it is called "Man-yana," tomorrow will do! It is called, *The drug of Indolence.* "Put off till tomorrow......!" Marijuana induces paranoia. It contains T. H. C.'s. It does not *regenerate* - it actually causes the brain to degenerate! For many who use this drug the lessons of will-power and responsibility are ignored. For others their lives are lived purely on the baser physical level. They may be on a journey but this is certainly not the journey to neutrality, illumination or liberation until they consciously change.

They need a crutch! They are not complete within the self. Will-power - the power of the conscious will - is not being used to overcome negative patterning from this lifetime or from previous incarnations and therefore slows down all positive achievement.

Proverbs. 15:32.

"He who ignores discipline despises himself, but whoever heeds correction, gains understanding.

There are those who are here to use their will-power for achievement on the physical and material plane. To create tangible reality! This is essential for evolution! Many young people find it easy not to work. They will not motivate and educate themselves for physical or academic achievement. Perhaps the work is not there but this does not prevent them from doing voluntary work. This gives them the ability to change the negative circumstances, ideals, ideas and attitudes in their lives. *Not trying* to transcend negative conditions will create negative karma. To change this attitude requires will-power! The ability to empower self! It is always easier to shift individual responsibilities to someone else.

It would be more beneficial if society could create work situations for those on unemployment benefits. There are many environmental and humanitarian elements which would benefit from the extra input. This would provide fresh circumstances and structures for our youth and our environment would definitely benefit also. The humanitarian spirit within us all especially our youth, must be encouraged - to help bring the massive changes needed to transform the consciousness of all humanity.

"Youth and love, sage and fool:
They all make their own reality."

The ability to empower self through positive means is a huge lesson for most of us! This is why it takes so long for some to complete the journey. For others it is easier not to try!

An example of: 'We always see what we don't have and never see what we do have and work with that.' is taken from Lobsang Rampa's book, 'Three Lives.'

"This very rich Lord of the manor was a womaniser. During the war he was called up for active service. While fighting he had his private parts shot off! He went home and could not function so decided the only thing he could do was to shoot himself. On the 'other side they wanted to know, 'why have you done this!' He was amazed. 'Why?' he explained in no uncertain terms, 'I could not live like this! I could not have women! I could not get married! I could not have children! My life was not worth living!' Then they said, 'What about your money, you could have created so much for humanity!'

> ***Unfulfillment is very often manifested through the misconception of our own human resources.***

So the next life this gentleman was born to very poor parents. He struggled and eventually became a doctor then worked in the slum areas helping the poor. What he had not created when he was rich he had now to create while he was poor.

Murder and suicide are definitely negative patterning from the past and will not be overcome until they are 'consciously' changed. Our whole existence on the earth plane is perpetuated through the imperfections of thoughts and deeds. To overcome to become is the journey of astute self-realisation. Most of us are here to work or we could not exist! Nonetheless each and every one of us has a spiritual mission - our own *personal transformation* to the higher realms of purified thoughts and deeds. How? It is only through strength and willpower we can take advantage of the many opportunities which present themselves everyday for our physical, emotional, mental and spiritual progress.

> ***"Your work is to discover your work,***
> ***then do it for all you are worth.***
> ***You can choose what you are!"***

Therefore willpower gives us the ability to create , to strive and to build, not just for ourselves but for all humankind. Not only to become motivated but to care. Through these concepts we conquer laziness, indolence and procrastination and this then gives us the clarity to *use* our energies to transform our lives. Individualisation gives us the power to transport ourselves to higher realms of awareness for all evolutionary growth and development and is the path to wisdom. Onward and upward we go as we continue our climb towards the light of personal achievement.

"The fulfilment of an action
depends on two factors -
destiny and human effort.
Destiny is the current manifestation
of the human efforts from past lives.
As a chariot cannot move with only one wheel,
destiny is not fulfilled without human effort.
People of wisdom and character
are devoted to action.
People without strength and conviction
depend on destiny.
Prosperity forsakes those
who rely on destiny
and favours those who act."

"The Way of Kings."
Ancient Wisdom from the Sanskrit Vedas.
Translated by Drew Lawrence.

CHAPTER 8

RESPONSIBILITY......... *"You can only be free,*

when you choose freedom.

It is an empty word without duty

and then you need love."

Responsibility is another of the important steps for reaching our freedom from the rounds of life, death and rebirth. Not only are we responsible for our decisions but for all the commitments we make. There are many social and humanitarian responsibilities which must be embodied throughout our spiritual journey to liberation as well as those of morality and integrity. The world seems to be full of individuals who are prejudiced, aggressive, too materialistic and those who simply just don't care. Then there are those who actually think they have reached their last life but are still bound by baser reality. So it becomes only too obvious why so many fail their Karmic responsibilities. It is only through self-awareness and the innate striving for purity of spirit which will finally create positive transformation and progress into the light. Of course we do not have to be perfect but we have to be aware.

"Anger, greed, needs, desires, heartaches
and the inability to motivate,
is what darkness is all about.

Seek to find truth and then to create,
whole new realities - of love, purity and faith!
This is our journey, to end our life.
To expanded consciousness, into the light."

Life is given to all of us so that we can grow, evolve and transcend. To eventually penetrate the illusions of the physical world and find the *'Absolute reality'*. Therefore we must all become responsible for who we are, where we are going and *how* we get there.

What about Hitler? Do you think he chose a life of evil while in the Heavenly Fields? No of course not. It was through his conscious reasoning ability that he journeyed on the path of darkness. His Destiny predetermined through the law of probability was the perpetuation of negative patterning and conditioning. This inevitability becomes more applicable with the handicap of childhood traumas created through past negative Karma. Nonetheless the law of probability can always be changed - this is choice!

Most of us have been a long time on the path to find liberation from the rounds of death and rebirth. There will always be those who will try to transform and regenerate themselves to higher spiritual consciousness through more purified thoughts and deeds. There are many who are dogmatic, rigid and biased with *the doors of the mind* closed to responsible and ethical behaviour. However they will still be a long time on the journey to expanded awareness! In the higher scheme of things they are not concerned as to how long it takes just that we all complete the journey. The laws of the Universe are fixed! The sooner we become responsible for all our choices and our actions the sooner we reach our ultimate destination - freedom and liberation from this ambulatory world of innate objectivity.

> ***"You will know what you are in time,***
> ***for consciousness evolves."***

Trish was a young mother and extremely motivated. Two disastrous relationships should have taught her the lesson of negative patterning created through need. He lifelong ambition was to become a Matron of a country hospital. To do this she had to start from the beginning. Trish decided to go back to school to study and eventually received the qualifications she needed to get her into University. Through her need to have another relationship she became involved with and married a man who was in jail. She believed in him completely and found renewed joy and hope in life as she fought to prove his innocence.

Being short of money she decided to get a job as a driver for 'the girls,' in an exclusive escort agency. Then she found out the truth about her husband! He had previously been convicted for the same type of sexual crimes he was now serving time for. The whole relationship was founded on lies, deception and fraud. Trish was completely devastated. When she had recovered after many tortuous months, she again became motivated through another relationship. This did not last very long because she decided not to be just employed as the agencies chauffeur but to become a paid escort herself. Her emotional instability turned her from a motivated loving individual to a life of promiscuity. Through her emotional insecurities, manifested by the desperate need to have someone in her life - she chose a path of negativity. Her dream of becoming a Matron had crashed even after completing a year at University. Her destiny, her karmic obligation this lifetime - to empower herself through strength, discernment, responsibility and *positive achievement.*

"If you faint in the day of adversity,
Your strength is small."

We must all be aware when we become negative through loss of direction, unhappiness, unfulfillment and even boredom it is very easy to create negative choices in our lives. Excitement, sensation, adventure and gratification seem to fill us with adrenaline. It is a human condition to want to revive ourselves but we must always try to create change through positive means. The repercussions from negative choices can sometimes seem incomprehensible especially when we are not even aware of the reasons for *life* in the first place.

"To try too hard, is as bad, as not hard enough.
To make music, the harp strings must be neither
too tight nor too slack."

Responsibility it seems is not a popular accomplishment. Lack of obligations seem to be the order of the day. How many times have you heard the statements, "He shirks his responsibility," or "It's not my responsibility," or "I don't want to become involved," and this one, "Let the Government take care of it." Then the Government itself seems to be helpless in meeting it's own obligations.

We are all responsible for our own actions! Too much responsibility can break anyone or anything. Too little breeds complacency, laziness, indolence and selfishness. Responsibilities must be met but be discriminating. We must all take responsibility for ourselves and this means for *all* the choices and commitments we make. Consequently we must think before we act!

There are those who have chosen a lifetime of responsibility and service to others to learn this valuable lesson. Caring for sick and aged parents or physically and mentally handicapped children are perfect examples.

Work, business and political enterprises, relationships, marriage and having children also teaches responsibility to a commitment. We all have different lessons to learn and problems to overcome. Becoming responsible for our choices will eventually lead to growth and positive Karma. However there is no need to become martyrs in any commitment or duty as this is useless self-sacrifice and lack of self-empowerment.

Many of the children who are mentally disabled, depending on the degree of disability have a valuable lesson to learn in individualisation and letting go of baser needs and desires. For the parents a lesson in responsibility! Some of these children have the ability to learn a tremendous amount.

The daughter of a friend has cerebral palsy but nevertheless has become quite proficient in many things. She was very excited with the delivery of her new computer. Her mother has given her a sense of independence and even a few lessons in responsibility through the many activities she is involved in.

Erin goes to dance classes, horse riding and as many other activities as she is able. Her mother does not allow her disability to restrict her to a life of complete and utter uselessness. Although she cannot account for herself completely during this lifetime there is much she can accomplish. My friend has chosen a life of tremendous responsibility and service. Karma - gives us all the opportunity to receive payments and pay debts. This is the law of cause and effect!

"All the world's a stage,
And all the men and women merely players."
Shakespeare's - As You Like It

Responsibility! Accountability! These are the karmic lessons for many of us, children as well as adults. In these days of Government assistance there are many individuals who fail to learn about obligation and responsibility. The exchange of a good day's work for a good day's pay should teach the lessons of accountability and discipline. For many in the western social structure - especially in Australia, the money comes without personal effort. This can create a difficult time for them in the future particularly when all monetary systems fail. When this time comes we will all have to stand on our own two feet. This will not be easy for anyone but a time when we must all nurture strength of spirit and universal love. Those who are able will accept responsibility to motivate, educate, enlighten, heal and care for the many who cross their path.

Proverbs: 11 : 24.

**"One man gives freely, yet grows all the richer;
Another withholds what he should give,
and only suffers want."**

Through the ability to voluntarily accept responsibility for humanity, comes evolutionary growth and positive Karma. This pathway brings with it a wonderful sense of freedom which helps us transcend the mediocrity of physical reality. This is because we can 'go beyond' our own importance which in turn brings an expansion of our higher capabilities. *'When we give our life we find it!'*

This unconditional giving should not come from the needs and desires motivated by self gain. This giving comes with true self-awareness, non-attachment, divine compassion, tolerance and understanding for all humankind. A very necessary step for "Crossing The Barrier To The Light Of Expanded Consciousness."

There is such a lack of accountability today not just for others but for ourselves. We see it in our cities and towns, we see it everywhere. The many cases of child abuse and molestation as well as the subjugation of war. There are those who destroy the environment and nature with graffiti and through the indiscriminate littering of roadsides and beaches. Environmental disasters, arson, chemical usage and nuclear warfare show a complete disregard for responsible humanitarian principles. Drug lords, drug abuse and violence create repercussions for those who build their lives on these foundations. Then there are those who participate in sexual promiscuity and perversion as well as those who mistreat animals. Last but not least there is the subject of bad manners. It does not matter how small the issue - it still shows lack of responsibility for our own actions.

Whatever rigid structures, ideals and attitudes from the past which fall for progress, our responsibility for morality and integrity should never change or even be questioned! Again teach - do not condemn. We will soon have the opportunity to break down many barriers for reform. This will not be a happy time for humankind but will bring the ability to create new belief systems, ideals, structures and philosophies which will be based on responsible action and love for all humanity.

"Optimism and kindness are rays of sunshine,
that don't cost a cent -
but give back the richest rewards,
that always seem to be 'heaven sent."

Through the preparation for change, reform and freedom which heralds the beginning of our New Age, humanity has failed in realising there is still room for good manners. Good manners are just good behavioural patterns which help us educate, communicate and assimilate with others. There is a blatant disregard for the feelings of others in the realisation of our own selfish needs and desires. Definitely to *'thine own self be true'* but also be ever aware we must not become like heavy machinery and completely run over everyone else in our attempt to empower ourselves.

᠁ The golden rule for all humanity - *'Do unto others as you would have them do unto you!'* It is such a pity we do not all use this philosophy in our every day life. If we did, there would be far less thoughtlessness and neglect for the elderly in our society? The many men and women who have served the community to the best of their ability and now that same society has no compassion, respect or need for their services.

It must of course be realised technology increases our capacities and we must move forward. However this does not mean we should forsake our laws of decency and integrity. Perhaps we should stop for awhile and take stock before thoughtlessness, rudeness and selfishness becomes too fashionable. There are many attributes to be shown towards the elderly, the two most important - respect and divine compassion.

Becoming responsible for actions and choices means we should be constantly aware of the law of Karma, the law of cause and effect. If we have lived our lives through selfishness or negative attitudes then we can guarantee 'what goes round does eventually come around.' It is extremely important to remember our own evolutionary and Karmic growth is not governed by the action of others but from our own actions.

NB.

Manners seem to be disregarded by many of us today but it is most notable in our youth. I have seen it on buses, trains, and in the street - just about everywhere. So many children fail to offer their seats to the elderly. They seem to think it is their divine right to empower themselves through selfish means. This is not what responsible living is about. Child or adult, we must become responsible for our own actions. This is why we are here in the first place. Our actions - all our actions - are being recorded for us to see - when we eventually leave the earth plane. Heaven does not have to judge - we do that with a little help from those in higher authority. What our spirit sees and understands is entirely different from our rational conscious mind. This is why so many individuals bring back guilt from previous lifetimes! The comprehension of what could have been accomplished previously, with a little more personal effort and responsible living.

Accountability for our own actions, for the commitments we make and for humanity is a huge step on the journey to freedom. Life is very complex but once we start taking responsibility for ourselves, for humankind and for our environment, we have crossed a huge barrier. This is not only true self-empowerment but also wisdom! The quote from the moon landing comes to mind.

"A small step for man,
but a giant leap for mankind."
(humankind)

Through the ability to empower self and then to use this energy with discrimination and responsibility comes mammoth changes to our social and environmental structures, to our humanitarian commitments and to ourselves.

"Better is a poor man who walks in his integrity
than a rich man who is perverse in his ways."

When we choose a life of wealth on the earth plane we are choosing one of responsibility. A life of wealth is always a life of being tested. To see what we can accomplish not only for ourselves but for the larger social structure. We are all being tested but especially when we are wealthy. There are many obligations and responsibilities for those with money! If we fill our lives with needs, desires and greed of the material world and negate our humanitarian obligations we are not on the right path. Look out - nurture love and divine compassion for humankind. But feeling is not enough we must all do something!

> ***"All paths lead to the same end.***
> ***All lives will lead to the same understanding."***

Giving the gifts of the spirit is *doing something*. Giving the gifts of the spirit does not necessarily mean money but time and energy. If we do not pass these tests we will repeat them in some future incarnation. Again we are not required to sacrifice or martyr ourselves but there are many Karmic obligations and responsibilities of a humanitarian nature which must be met.

> ***"Some will grow more powerful, richer.***
> ***But if a person gets too rich without sharing -***
> ***Like an overripe fruit they will fall."***

When we take on any commitment we must honour and fulfil the task to the best of our ability. This is Karma! We do not have to take this to the extreme. There are those who have such a great sense of obligation to authority and fail to see their social and family responsibilities. This very often creates havoc not only in their own life but in the lives of others. One case comes to mind:

The explorer, Matthew Flinders was captured and taken prisoner by the French. (England and France were at war) He was not put in prison but allowed to roam the Island at his leisure. So he "gave his word" not to escape - and he didn't! He remained there for seven years even though he could have left if he had so desired. Meanwhile at home his wife whom he loved dearly, lay very ill. His word and his sense of responsibility was not to Annette his wife to whom he had made a commitment but to his captors.

This is responsibility taken to the extreme. No doubt in some future lifetime he would have Karmic obligations and responsibilities to Ann, (as he called her) which had to be repaid. This is definitely not punishment but a chance to give back and to become responsible for what he had failed to honour in the first place. Karma will eventually lead us all to higher understanding of the universal laws.

Another example, taken from a wonderful and enlightened book which I sincerely recommend for everyone. Joe Fisher and Dr. Joel Whitton's, "Life Between Life." (Harper Collins - Publishers Ltd)

A patient in past life regression found himself back two lifetimes. He was married with two children and had a mistress with whom he had two children also. When he died he provided for his wife and children but to the mistress and their children he left nothing. By the simple act of having a mistress in the first place he had made a commitment! He had failed his responsibilities. This lifetime he is a very conscientious and loving husband to that very same woman. There were no Karmic ties with the previous wife this incarnation.

"Karma is the link, in the chain of life."

Karma is the law of cause and effect from one lifetime to the next. It is responsibility! It is achievement internal and external. Everything we do will be seen. This is the only way we will comprehend the 'Universal Laws'. The ability to pay debts and receive payments. This is justice! Divorce and separation are fine as long as they are resolved as amicably as possible. The commitment has been broken. Children must be catered for in any dissolution of marriage, but many man made laws demand extreme action. Greed has no part in the responsibilities we owe to others. In fact greed will always create negative Karma until we reverse these energies through our conscious thought patterns.

While children are still dependent, parents must always honour their commitments - their responsibilities through love and divine compassion. Knowing the law of Karma should make us *think* before we act. Children should always become responsible for who and what they are through the *positive* guidance of parents and teachers.

Not to listen to advice and to ignore the good intentions of others with complete disregard and blatant hostility is poor judgment.

Wisdom comes from experience. Children must have boundaries, there must be right and wrong - true and false. Our lessons are to overcome all the negative patterns in our lives in favour of the positive. To ignore boundaries, laws, discipline, commitments and responsibilities means we bury our heads in the sand.

Boundaries are essential when building strength of character, awareness and wisdom. Children do not have the experience and wisdom to lead. They are here to learn - as we all are. Children must be taught and as parents we all take on the responsibility and commitment to do just that. Especially do not try and develop the divine child syndrome. Love, care, uplift and inspire by all means but through indulgence the *divine child* centres on self and does not look to help humanity.

Proverbs: 19:20

**"Listen to advice and accept instruction,
that you may gain wisdom for the future."**

Responsibility seems to be the most obligatory undertaking we will all have to experience in our lives at one time or another. This applies to children as well as adults. As I have said before, most of us choose our parents either through negative or positive Karma. Therefore if there are problems in early childhood with parents there are definitely reasons why we choose these obstacles! Perhaps there are those who have been abusive in previous lives or those who have misused their sexuality. Sometimes the lesson may be 'self-empowerment' and therefore we have to learn individualisation and the ability to stand alone even as a child.

A client had a past life regression and discovered she had been a prisoner of war. To help appease the guards she used her sexuality to win their favours. This lifetime her childhood was very unhappy and traumatic because of incest. Why would this happen? We must not misuse our sexuality to compromise our integrity even in war. If we use our sexuality to gain what we want from others - others can use their sexuality to gain what they want from us. This is justice! Clearly we must eventually liberate ourselves from all physical manifestations and deceptions of our earthly existence.

Seems hard and cruel? Remember Karma is cause and effect! The earth plane is where we come to change, to learn and to transcend. This is our earth school not heaven! Reincarnation gives us the ability to transform ourselves through the *Conscious mind* and then the *Conscious will.* Heartache and pain purifies the soul consciousness. Physical manifestations are not the *true reality.* Needless to say the more we evolve to higher consciousness the more we can understand these esoteric truths.

> *"Today I work through the celestial light,*
> *To create abundance, success and a happy life."*

As a child Sally had problems with her mother who was very abusive. Through her mothers frustrations over money and problems in her own relationship Sally and her brother became the victims. Sally was able through past life regression to access a past life where she knew her mother. In this past life, Sally was a young man and her mother a young woman. She saw herself standing over this cowering, frightened young woman yelling, "I don't want you, get out of my life. I don't want you! I don't need you! Get out - get out! I never want to see you again!" She was also able to see what eventually happened to this young woman. She became an emotional cripple!

So we can see why there are so many negative patterns we keep repeating. The lack of empowerment is a major stumbling block for many. This will always become repeated conditioning over many lifetimes if we do not use our will-power to 'overcome to become.' Her mother is still trying to empower herself because of the patterns and conditioning from past lives. She has tried lesbianism and even developed breast cancer in this lifetime! This shows the inability to find balance within herself. The acceptance of her own feminine and masculine energies created from the patterning and conditioning not just from her last life but also from her previous incarnations. 'The inability to believe in and nurture herself!'

For Sally it showed her that in all her lifetimes she had experienced as a man she had always abused her power. We do not have to resort to cruelty to justify our actions and to find empowerment. Sally is now a tremendous support to her Mother because she can understand the reasons behind all the negative patterns and conditions in her life. She has even helped her Mother to believe in and empower herself!

Unconditional love for self is the first golden rule. *Do unto others, as you would have them do unto you* - is the next. The sooner we understand and use these philosophies everyday the sooner we can leave the earth plane permanently.

"Cleverness learns something.
Wisdom gives up some certainty everyday."

Those who have leadership positions must have and uphold a responsibility to humanity. To abuse positions of trust is a very grave act indeed. There are so many cases of men and women in positions of authority using and abusing their power for their own gain - for material gain, for power, for position, for sex and for evil.

The Golden age will bring responsible living for much of humanity. Eventually not too far into the 21st. Century there will be no more killing through war. This is only on a civilisation level - personal Karma is again choice. Peace will reign! When individuals kill because of duty they come back the next lifetime or in future lifetimes to give to humanity through their healing, transformative, regenerative and creative energies or through their social and humanitarian responsibilities. No one is being punished they just have to reverse the energies of actually taking life. This is their Karmic responsibility! Those who create and delight in aggression, tyranny, hate, torture and persecution, will always reap the consequence of negative actions! Karma is always in existence!

> *"Good and bad may be true,*
> *but if bad, one must try to change it."*

Murder is another story. Murderers come into this life with the probability they will murder again - until they consciously change. A case in point. The Charles Manson story - and the women who followed him: These three women were actually sentenced to die and at the last moment the death sentence was abolished. Their sentence was commuted to life imprisonment. One of these women admitted to having stabbed a victim sixteen times and feeling no remorse.

When they were interviewed after the trial these women were not sorry for what they had done or for the murders they had committed. Thirty years after the trial they had changed their conscious thought patterns and knew what they had done was wrong! They had reversed their way of thinking! If they had been put to death after the crimes they would have had to come back next life with the probability of repeating the same patterns until they *consciously* changed. This is Karma!

We must all accept responsibility for the choices we make! These women have still not let go of guilt and still believe they have a 'bad seed' within them. This is how they rationalise why they killed in the first place. This means they will come back next lifetime with feelings of guilt which will again have to be overcome. Through the ability to change our conscious reasoning, comes greater understanding of our Karmic responsibilities not only to ourselves, but for all humankind. Onward and upwards we climb towards the light of infinite wisdom

An Ancient Eastern Philosophy:

"Why is there evil?
Perhaps because,
good is not good,
until it is chosen."

CHAPTER 9

DISCRIMINATION......   *"He who lacketh discrimination, whose*

mind is unsteady and whose heart is

impure, never reacheth the goal,

but is born again and again.

But he who hath discrimination,

whose mind is steady and whose heart

is pure, reacheth the goal and having

reached it, is born no more."

Katha Upanishad.

This is one of the most important steps for expansion into the higher realms of consciousness, for freedom and for enlightenment. When I talk about discrimination I do *not* mean prejudice, unfairness, judgment, victimisation, persecutory or puritanical actions. Discrimination means discernment, discretion, insight, penetration, refining, distinguishing, clear-sightedness, to know chalk from cheese, to know the difference. The ability to see through illusion!

Too many spiritual seekers are not using their discriminative powers in their search for spirituality. Spirituality comes from within, it is not found 'out there!' To find the keys to self-awareness and motivation you may certainly have to educate yourself through therapy, courses, lectures, books and seminars. With so many of the avenues which are available it is imperative we use our powers of discrimination to help us sift the rubbish and illusion from the truth. There are many *so called* spiritual experts out there who are taking your money and they have nothing to sell! Discriminate - discern!

A client remarked he had been advised by a clairvouant, it was dangerous to astral travel because someone could take over his body. This is definitely not so! When you astral travel you are *not* disconnected from your physical body but still connected through your silver cord and therefore prevents anyone or anything from taking over the physical body. It is only through death this silver cord is severed.

If more people would learn to astral travel consciously to the *higher dimensions* there would be more understanding and unconditional love for others. Of course - discrimination must always be exercised, even in the astral plain. Through the power of negative thought which includes fear, the elementals can create whatever we think. Remember we are magnets! There is nothing to fear but fear itself! Through positive self-empowerment, physically, emotionally, mentally and spiritually, which is really what faith is all about we can create our own protection.

A friend was told she had three million entities on her phone and more in her healing room! This particular gentleman told her it would cost a very large sum of money to cleanse her room. This is illusion! Through *positive self-empowerment* we can all negate the negativity around us. Through our own divine power of positive thoughts and love we create positive energies within ourselves as well as without. Positive thoughts attract positive energies negative thoughts attract negative energies.

This means we all have the ability to heal and cleanse ourselves through our positive faith in self. This faith is our own divine power!

In the past there were always those who could bring fear and death through curses and black magic. Why? Through superstition and negativity people believed this was possible! If one believes so can one create! Through our *positive thoughts* we create a barrier around us that protects us from outside influences. This barrier is our Aura! If we are negative the Aura does not become as energised or powerful as it should be and can allow negative thoughts to penetrate. Evolutionary growth gives us all the ability to transcend the negativity which fear, superstition, ignorance, ritual and dogma creates.

Please empower yourselves through positive thoughts, love and faith. All my friend has to do to cleanse her healing room is to surround herself with positive thoughts, love and believe in her own divine power. This is faith! Beautiful stones, incense as well as relaxation music and aromatic oils can energise and balance the room and create an oasis of peace and harmony. Positive affirmations if repeated over and over will definitely uplift our psyche and create an immeasurable effect on our day to day existence.

> *"Today I seek wisdom to lighten the way,*
> *today I seek joy to brighten my day."*

How many clairvoyants have you seen and have told you about your guides? Well how do you know they are your guides? Is it because you were told or because the guides themselves told you?

Can you prove it?

No you can't! There are many spirits and elementals on the other side who will hang onto those who need them and those who believe in them. They will pretend they are anyone you want them to be. If you want Cleopatra, St. Joan or St Germain you will find them. Even if you want and believe in angels you will see them. You can manifest anything you want in the spirit world through thought. This is because we are all like magnets and as you know magnets attract. Through the power of faith - we can create from the etheric substance in the universe anything we want to believe in.

This is power of thought!

That is the illusion! What would Cleopatra, St Joan or St Germain be doing 'out there' anyway. Remember Karma? By now, through the continual round of death and rebirth they would definitely not be who they were in previous lifetimes anyway. Even if they had reached liberation from life on earth they would not be hanging around on the earth plane by choice. This is why we must open the doors of the mind - through the power of discrimination.

Are we negating our own spiritual growth through these ambiguous modes of spirituality? Are we using our powers of discrimination and discernment for the expansion of our *own* consciousness? What do we need guides for anyway? Why not just have a direct link to your higher self? It is like a direct telephone line versus the party line. The direct link is just that but the party line is where we have a lot of interference in trying to reach the *source*. Develop your own power through astral travelling or meditation.

This is *not* the path to discriminating wisdom. Neutrality comes when we have learnt to let go - when we know how to go beyond - to transcend - then we have the ability to empower ourselves through the wisdom of discrimination. When we actually astral travel consciously to the higher planes we do not need to channel or to have guides anyway.

The great spiritual Masters or Teachers (so named because of the opening of the Kundalini Power) do not believe in guides or have the need to contact the world of spirits from the lower realms. Their ultimate attainment is enlightenment and illumination. This comes through their own spiritual empowerment! Remember when we find our freedom and liberation from this the physical realm our spirit would not want to come back here. This is baser physical reality!

Hanging on to anything including guides is a classic case of not being empowered! *Hang onto yourself! Empower yourself!* Cross the barrier to the light of *Expanded Consciousness*. Hanging on to anyone from the other side is an extremely selfish and confined existence. Poor Elvis! How can he possibly be reborn as another identity when so many people hang onto his memory? He can't! You must know what it feels like when someone hangs onto you continually? Well that is what it is like when we hang onto someone on the other side. Hanging onto the departed creates tortured souls. They have really *gone home* to the heavenly fields and yet we in the mortal world need to hold on. This will always drag them back. Earth is not home! Set them free! Our departed loved ones will still *visit us* voluntarily, to give love and comfort whenever we go through times of heartache and conflict.

Has humanity changed so much from the ancient civilisations of 'many Gods' to now, when we can contact our 'many guides.' We could almost have one for every day of the week. Which one will I contact today? Recently a gentleman told me he had six guides around him to protect him! Protect him? What about his own power? What benefit are guides if we already possess the power to protect ourselves? Do guides bring happiness? What happens to free will? Does it make individuals feel more spiritual? This is *not* true spirituality! Spirituality comes from within and is the evolutionary growth of our conscious mind. If we need guides it gives us excuses not to grow, to evolve, to transform and to transcend.

Perhaps there are those who need guides to feel more secure as many of these people are still in conflict and cannot find direction in their lives. This is definitely not self empowerment! It is not expanded consciousness or true spirituality! It is certainly not enlightenment or revelation and it is not illumination or neutrality!

Sometimes when clairvoyants see these images around you it is very often the images of who you were in past lives and not guides. This is why you should never really believe in what you *think* you see. The power of thought creates, it visualises, it manifests, it perceives, it imagines, it illusions and it deceives.

"The way is not in the sky: it is in your heart."

Two stories which emphasise lack of discrimination with the spirit world.

A clairvoyant had drawn a picture of the guide she saw around my friend. She took this picture home and showed her girlfriend who then fainted.

When she regained conscoiusness, explained, " that's my mother!" No doubt the departed mother couldn't communicate with her daughter so decided the next best thing would be to try her daughter's friend. We must all use discrimination in all our choices and our judgments.

Discrimination must be achieved before we can find truth and enlightenment. There are many spirits in the astral world which we do not comprehend or understand so it is wise to leave them alone. We must become empowered through our own abilities.

A very dear friend told me a man came up to her at the Spiritualist Church she attends, who was clairvoyant. He gave her the names of the two guides he felt were around her. She was quite bewildered as she does not believe in or need guides but the names were very familiar. Later that evening she picked up the book she had been reading and continued from where she had left off. Then she laughed! There were the two names of her so called guides, the main characters of the book. My friend is extremely clairvoyant and has seen in my home, my father and daughter Marrianne who have departed to *the other side.*

There are many ways to contact the spirits. Many get impressions, some are from telepathic images and others from clairvoyant ability. So at times the images may be misconstrued and jumbled. This is why discrimination is essential for processing all information which comes through. To really know what is truth and what is illusion and misinformation. This is the reason it can become so chaotic. There are many spirits on the other side! Astrals who have left the confines of the earthly body for awhile as well as departed souls.

There are also those who can be manifested simply through the power of thought. We are all magnets and the more we need and believe in them the more we attract! Then there are those so called spirits who are only the remains of the etheric double from the physical bodies of vibrant individuals who have left the earth plane. Their spirit has gone to the heavenly fields but their image stays on this plane in the etheric double. This image has all the appearance of these long departed souls and can even be contacted.

So we must all be aware but we must also question! We are all on a journey of evolutionary growth so how far have some of these spirits progressed? Because they are in spirit form they will be able to comprehend the astral plane better than those in the physical body which is to be expected. There are as many levels of astral planes as there are levels of evolutionary growth on the earth plane. The majority of these spirits will still not be able to comprehend divine knowledge since they have still not progressed to higher dimensions than this the physical realm. Take control of your own life through your own self-empowerment. Through the ability to astral travel consciously one can go beyond the lower realm of spirit to much higher dimensions of spiritual reality. This always depends on personal growth and the degree of spiritual comprehension. We are what we believe!

Is your reality guides or channelling? Ask yourself, "Are these procedures true spirituality, fads, cult practices or crutches?" This is not the path to the light of expanded consciousness, liberation or enlightenment. There may be knowledge but it is not *divine knowledge or revelation*. Perhaps the lesson here is to learn to believe in your own power by empowering yourself! To transcend the need and desire to hang onto all the enigmatic forms of the spirit world. These unnecessary practises will not bring growth. In fact they create illusion and many misconceptions in our lives. We are here to evolve, to regenerate and to transform ourselves on the journey to the light.

The ability to expand consciousness to enlightenment and revelation will bring divine knowledge through your own power. You then become a vessel for higher truths. This is certainly *not* through channelling! There have been many who have reached this exalted state through the opening of the Kundalini power. These enlightened ones have taken many, many years of denial and even pain, not just to open up this force - but to learn to control and use this majestic power through the purity of mind, heart and deed. Those who don't can actually die or end in asylums - because they cannot control this tremendous force and energy the right way, *through pure positive thought and action.*

The purpose for all of us? "Seek only truth and we will find truth!" We must all use our discriminative faculties to distinguish between cultish practices and true spirituality. There is so much phenomena in the universe we simply do not possess the power to comprehend it all. To recognise our limitations is not denial of it's existence. There are many more important issues to recognise and understand. Evolutionary growth and development is the only true reason we are on the earth plane in the first place. Our journey - the journey for each and everyone of us - to cross the barrier to the light of expanded consciousness! To believe in the occult does not necessarily mean we are spiritual. Remember true spirituality comes from within it is the way we *live* our lives through truth, love, light and faith.

"The essence of all things is one and the same,
perfectly calm and tranquil, and shows no sign
in 'becoming'. Ignorance, however is in its
blindness and delusion, oblivious of Enlightenment
and on that account, cannot recognise truthfully,
all those conditions, differences and activities
which characterize the phenomena of the Universe."

Ashvaghosha........

The ability to penetrate physical reality to find the realms of infinite wisdom comes through the ability to discriminate. Sappho the Greek Poetess was born on the Island of Lesbos, approximately 2,600 years ago. (The Ioanian culture) It was here the husbands encouraged lesbianism so the wives would not become entangled with other men, while they were away at sea. Many lesbians make a pilgrimage to Lesbos every year and honour her statue. Why?

In the past she was honoured and imitated for her poetry and her knowledge. But why honour her now for the very thing she undoubtly needed to transcend? Her sexual practices! She has probably had many lifetimes since, learning, overcoming, growing and evolving, on her journey to the light. We all have! This is Karma!

"Although they are only breath,
words which I command, are immortal."

Sappho................

Remember we are the sum total of *all* our existences not just one lifetime! This is our evolutionary Karmic reward! Who are these people honouring - the past or ignorance? When we have eventually transcended all earthly misconceptions we would not need to go back to the past to be recognised for negative patterns and conditions. Our Karmic reward is through transformation and the ability to find our freedom from the past.

Enlightened souls always travel towards the light. Hero worship is lack of empowerment. Your own self-empowerment brings you to honouring yourself. The hero you wish to believe in lies within yourself. Discrimination will give us all the ability to find the truth - to distinguish - to discern - to penetrate illusion and delusion and the ability to know the difference. *This is wisdom!*

> **"Each moment is possible only because of
> every moment since the beginning of time.
> Now it is here! Each moment is thus inevitable
> and to no-ones fault or credit."**

Homosexuality is an extremely controversial subject but I feel I must touch on it a little. Interestingly again 2,600 years ago homosexuality was the order of the day. Today, it seems people are again trying to condone and accept wrong sexual practices. They call this freedom of choice! Perhaps it is only the path of least resistance! What about our integrity, our morality and spiritual responsibilities? It takes a great deal of discernment to see truth and even more to achieve wisdom!

It is not the love which is wrong, it is the sexual practices. This is *sodomy*! This is baser sexual energy! This is not judgment - just truth! There are those of us who have trodden that very same pathway in previous lifetimes. The lessons for each and every one of us are the same! To transcend our baser energies! This is why we are here in the first place! Many would argue love between two consenting adults is not wrong and the need to express this love through sex is freedom of expression.

What about incest? Is this right. No? Therefore it stands to reason there are wrong and right sexual practices! Expanded consciousness brings the ability to transcend the baser levels of physical reality. The pathway for progress and knowledge is through the control of the five senses for regeneration. Through truth, knowledge and the ability to discern.

If this is your reality you do not have to fill your life with guilt or fear. If you can change - change. If you can't change or do not want to change - fine. Karma is choice! It is free will. Consciousness will always evolve, eventually. If you have already had eight lives to get you to this incarnation you will most probably have a few more lives to transcend this baser physical reality. The choice is yours!

The number of lives we have is of course determined by our needs, desires, abilities and our capacity to transcend the misconceptions of the physical world to a higher realm of understanding and expanded consciousness. It is not gauged by the laws of man but the laws of the Divine. The laws of the universe do not change. We do! When we make excuses for expanding individuality and spirituality we should not let go of the laws of morality and integrity to do so! Fashion and indulgence do not dictate our laws of decency!

The rejection of opposites means we reject the balance within ourselves. We must create balance within to create balance without. If we renounce the masculine *or* feminine energies within ourselves then we also renounce them without. When any of us lose direction because we reject our own sexuality through negative means we will always have to sort it out in future incarnations.

This does not include those who seek the denial of sexual partnerships in pursuit of higher spiritual expansion. When monks deny sexual expression they are utilising that energy to expand the higher chakras. This of course, can even happen through the sexual act but only when men and women have reached a higher dimension of spiritual expansion. (Not through sodomy!)

This rejection of opposites is also another reason why there is so much cruelty, aggression, hate, manipulation, tyranny, suppression and sickness in the world today. To accept our masculine and feminine energies within means we accept them without! This is the only true pathway to equality!

Spirituality - is this our ultimate attainment? There are many levels of spirituality. There are many devoted monks who have had at least five lifetimes as monks. One can be spiritual and still come from baser energies. Spirituality alone is not the key to immortality of the spirit - to liberation. Evolutionary growth demands the transcendence of all baser energies, physically, emotionally, mentally and spiritually. This is expanded consciousness! This is wisdom!

*"Only those who dare NOT give up their beliefs,
because they have no wisdom - will insist that others believe
as they do."*

The power of discrimination brings the need to question! Change and expansion does not mean we throw away the laws of morality, responsibility and discernment and become over expansive and indulgent. The Laws of the Universe do not change!

We are here to open the doors of the mind to truth and light. This means we must expand the mind to encompass love, truth and faith. To transcend the encapsulation of our earthly desires through a love which regenerates not degenerates. It is not the love which is wrong but the sexual practices. These sexual practices do not regenerate they actually degenerate. We do not hate - we do not condemn - we do not suffer guilt. Karma will always bring the ability for evolutionary growth - to change our patterning and conditioning. Through the many, many lifetimes of life, death and rebirth we will all have the opportunity to overcome to become and transcend the deceptions of the purely physical world.

"The world is a trap for fools; only he who SEES goes free."

The physical world is a purely false realm. It has no *absolute reality* behind it because it is only a transitory world. A world which we will all eventually outgrow. This may take many lifetimes but change we will until we can reach the higher dimensions of profound wisdom.

Numerologically *'Gay'* vibrates to 15/6. In the Tarot, this is symbolised by *'The Devil.'* This is limitation and bondage or freedom the choice is yours! The ability to control the animal nature from the illusions and sdeceptions of physical reality. To find our ultimate freedom from the encapsulation of our baser physical and emotional energies to a much higher realm of *love consciousness.* The word *AIDS* has the very same meaning!

As I have said before there are many grades of spirituality! Just because we understand the occult or have read books on esoteric knowledge, does not automatically make us spiritual. This attitude can definitely bring limitation and bondage into our lives. This mentality can bring with it denial of further growth and development. What is true Spirituality? It is the expansion and knowledge of the spirit through our own Karmic and evolutionary growth. The ability to live our lives through *truth*! Through *faith*! Through *love and divine compassion* and through *wisdom*!

> **"Get away from life-lust, from conceit,**
> **from ignorance and from distractions craze:**
> **Sunder the bonds; so only shalt thou**
> **come to utter, end of ill.**
> **Throw off the chain of birth and death -**
> **thou shalt knowest what they mean -**
> **So free from craving, in this life on earth.**
> **Thou shalt go on thy way, calm and serene."**
> *Psalms of the Early Buddhists.*
> *(Mrs Rhys David's Translation)*

Our third chakra is the chakra of reason and discrimination. It is golden yellow, the colour of intelligence - of wisdom. An experiment was made on a class of school children. Three walls were painted yellow and the back wall was painted blue. (This was the wall the teacher was facing) After one year the children's I. Q. was raised by a substantial percentage - something like 12%. We must all open and use this chakra for the ability to reason, distinguish and to discriminate. Many clairvoyants have their third eye chakra opened but not the chakra of discrimination. They have the ability to see but not to discern!

Discrimination! What a powerful tool. It brings insight, peace and understanding. It gives us the clarity and wisdom for individualisation. It creates the leaders and not the followers. It is true self-empowerment because when we have the ability to discern we do not need to follow others. It is the catalyst for neutrality and liberation. Illumination is impossible without discrimination. It makes possible the expansion of the higher chakras for truth and revelation - and I do not mean channelling. (In fact many individuals who channel lack discrimination.) It is also interesting to note - one of the petals of personality of the heart chakra (fourth chakra) which must be mastered before it can pulsate in all its power is that of discrimination.

There are those who operate entirely from the third Chakra of discrimination and have not developed or opened their higher Chakras. These are the individuals who are so discerning and logical they cannot see anything unless they can touch it or rationalise it's existence. They have tunnel vision and have not opened their higher mind to include spiritual truths, light, love and faith for expanding consciousness.

A few years ago my daughter went missing. A friend thought it would be a good idea to visit a woman who could channel the spirit realm. She was supposedly genuine because it was reputed she sometimes helped the police. Though reluctant I decided it couldn't hurt and agreed to go. The woman started to channel through my friend whom she had put into a trance. She received the messages from the other side, "that my daughter was dead"! They said, "She had been raped and was lying in a deserted house somewhere." Now if I had lacked discrimination I would have believed her and no doubt been very upset, even hysterical.

I beleive I am, 'discernment personified.' I just knew this was not true! In fact three days later my daughter was found safe and well in another state. It was the first anniversary of her elder sister's death and it had created heartache, illusion and therefore little rationalisation. Today I'm happy to say, she has overcome these traumas and is the proud mother of two beautiful children.

"We all need help to change and grow."

So you can see how easy it is to create through the spirit world and through the power of the mind whatever one wants. Be aware, not only channelling but even hypnosis can be an unreliable source of information. I would certainly warn everyone that they should take care and only attend consultations with qualified medical practitioners of hypnosis. We cannot see truth unless we can discriminate.

This is one of the most powerful lessons there is! Certainly one which is the catalyst not only for liberation but for enlightenment. When we surround ourselves with negativity or undesirable realities it is impossible to see the truth. We become immersed in a sea of distorted perceptions of right and wrong. The light goes out!

"The way is simple but simplicity is not stupidity:
It needs awareness. A youth who leans carelessly
over a cliff is a fool. A mountain standing
above an abyss stays calm: It is in it's right place."

Many concern themselves with body consciousness and believe a healthy body creates a healthy mind. In fact it is the reverse which is actually true. A healthy mind creates a healthy body. Through the continual and almost fanatical preoccupation with the perfect body image, through media hype we are creating too much body consciousness. By all means look after yourself and your body but this can be taken to extremes. We can become trapped on this level and become encased in physical reality.

These ideals very often create vanity. Vanity is an illusion! Transcend the physical - the body and expand the mind! Of course a certain amount of discipline is definitely good for everyone! Be careful, always take the middle path and do not allow discipline to go to extremes. Very often this pathway creates obsessions, sickness, rigidity and many misconceptions. Then vanity becomes another illusion which must be broken.

It is only through the mind that we can tap into a higher perceptivity. The control of the mind gives us the ability to create positive thoughts and conditions in our lives. Therefore it enables us to transcend the physical and to elevate our thought processes into higher realms of consciousness. This then gives us the ability to journey into expanded dimensions of reality to find neutrality, illumination, and a far greater knowledge than body consciousness.

I certainly believe some forms of exercise and metaphysical disciplines are good for you, (Yoga, Tai Chi, Chi Kung) if *not* taken to extremes. Be careful, through some forms of yoga we can open our higher chakras through the Kundalini power. It is only when we have achieved *discrimination with discipline* physically, emotionally, mentally and spiritually we can even begin to become pure in mind, heart and deed and are able to handle such majestic energy and power. This power is not to be used by the novice! You are playing with fire and as they say, those who play with fire get burned. This can actually happen and unless you know what to do through years of training you may not live to tell the tale. (Re - Gopi Krishna's book - Kundalini)

There are many who believe higher spirituality forbids the use of meat in our diet. This may be true for those monks who spend most of their time in retreat for meditation but for most of us meat in moderation actually *grounds us,* it keeps our feet on the ground, which of course is why we are here in the first place! (It doesn't have to be red meat - white meat will suffice) The total lack of meat very often creates an imbalance of mind, body and spirit. Until we have transcended all physical reality. It certainly may cleanse the body but what about the purification of the mind? This must come through Karmic and Evolutionary growth!

To kill an animal for food is not cruel, in fact the spirit leaves the body almost instantly. On the other hand plants make much more agonizing sounds when they are harvested. If we could hear them naturally we may never eat fruit or vegetables again!

All extremes are wrong.
Our journey is
through the golden middleway!

Discrimination brings clarity and this in turn brings the ability to know and understand truth. So many misinterpret truth to their own realisations and understanding. True and false, illusion and reality, the meaning of life? These are the questions! However without discrimination our perception becomes too expansive and imaginative - we cannot distinguish or discern. On the other hand those who come from too much discrimination are so logical and rational they cannot see higher truth! Cosmic truth does not change - we do. The laws of the universe are fixed!

"Heaven does not judge.
We judge ourselves
and this is a difficult and dangerous thing to do:
It is difficult, for we will stand on our heads
to see that we are right
and it is dangerous,
for we know, wemust be wrong
and are angry with ourselves.
The difficult and dangerous must be faced however,
but with strength and gentleness together;
no extremes, but the middle way.

"What is truth? Well there is our own truth which is gauged on our perception, comprehension and understanding of available knowledge, insight and the many phenomena of the Universe. Then there is Universal Truth! It is only through the ability to discriminate - to sift - to discern that we can reach a higher understanding and perception of right and wrong, true and false, illusion and reality. Many religious fanatics believe they have found truth and lead their followers to suicide. The 'holy wars,' were supposed to be fought in the name of truth! Many give themselves to a life of suppression and dogma in the name of spiritual truth also. Then there are those who are supposed to be channelling so called higher truths through divine deities.

Is this what many perceive as truth? Yes, this is only the truth of the individuals concerned. They have not discerned or discriminated because they come from *their own perception of truth - not from wisdom.* We can always create what we want to believe in - that is faith! Very soon humanity will have truth and knowledge through the teachings of a new Divine Leader and his disciples, certainly not through channelling but through his presence on earth.

The purpose of the next age - the Age of Aquarius, is to know Universal Truth and to use it with Humanitarian love for the unity of all humankind. One religion and one race of people! This will bring many eruptions for change - which is symbolic of Uranus the ruler of Aquarius. We will all have to let go of our many cultures, ideals, beliefs, patterning and conditioning for the unification of all humanity. This, then creates the catalyst for our last age 2000 years from now.

"Of those who seek the light,
the wisest knows that each night
is followed by a day
and a day by a night - forever!"

There are many women who live with guilt, fear, heartache and torment because of abortion. This is *not* wrong if the abortion takes place in the early stages of the pregnancy. "This is a human life you are killing," anti-abortionists say. "You are a murderer!" *This is not so!* Until the spirit enters the new baby - it is incomplete. If it was born without the spirit - it would die anyway! The spirit does not enter the body through the silver cord until just before the birth itself. Perhaps a little earlier for some but certainly not in the early stages of the pregnancy.

This is not murder - it is not wrong - it is not a sin! There is too much heartache, guilt and even chaos caused through the authoritarian figures who set themselves up as Gods in their judgments and perceptions of what is right for the women involved. No doubt if men became pregnant the law would be changed and abortion would be accepted by all. It is time for change! Religious dogma, prejudice, lack of knowledge, rigid and unrealistic moral views bring confined circumstances, limitation and bondage into our lives. Of course to prevent the need for abortion in the first place all men and women should become more aware of their responsibilities and commitments. Education is the catalyst for all progress and change. Prevention is always better than cure.

"The wise of heart is called a man of discernment."

Unlock the doors of the mind - expand the consciousness. Use discrimination and you will find your freedom. Everything we do - our choices in life will ultimately come back to the self. We must all become responsible for our own life. Without the ability to discriminate - to discern - to distinguish, how can we make the right choices - the right decisions? We may of course need to listen to others for advice and wisdom but in the end we are still responsible for ourselves. Truth with the discrimination to see it will always set us free.

> *"Discrimination and control brings freedom,*
> *peace, harmony and contentment into our lives.*
> *Room to fill our minds and hearts with*
> *beauty, light, love and faith and then*
> *because we are able to see beauty and love,*
> *we can also see ourselves."*

RE Magnets of the Universe

PART 3

FREEDOM

CHAPTER 10

MEDITATION... "*All things were chaos until mind*

came to set them in order."

Said a 6th. Century Philosopher from Ionia:

Meditation is a discipline - a mind discipline; the technique we use to purify our thought processes; a means of exploring the inner-self; a communion with the spirit; contemplation and the vehicle or consciousness we use to transcend all earthly concerns;

From the very moment of birth we learn to identify with everything around us. Our mind is our power house of operations. To live and exist in the physical body - to learn, to evolve and to become responsible for ourselves - we have to think. So many thoughts! Every day we organise and construct not only our own lives but the lives of others.

So much to see - so much to do! An incessant round of happenings, ideas, attitudes and thought patterns. Self-awareness is when we start to contemplate the who and what we are - the meaning of life. When we start to investigate we must go within to explore the inner-self, the soul. Meditation becomes the means to feed our spirit and to find the seeds of life. It is the mental discipline we use to purify our thought processes to find peace, tranquillity and the release or control of pain. Meditation acts as the bridge connecting the mental and spiritual realms and is the vehicle we use to transcend the physical plane to the divine. Through establishing this practice every day we are able to find serenity, discipline and greater expansion, on our journey to the light.

Proverbs:27:19.

**"As in water, face answers to face,
so the mind of a man, reflects the man."**

There are many stages of meditation, the first four dealing with the realm of form and the last four dealing with the formless. The first four deal with worldly manifestations and the latter deals with the transcendence of all earthly concerns.

The last stages of meditation do not require *nothingness* as some people believe but projects us beyond earthly ambiguity which will eventually lead to the exalted state of neutrality. The transcendence of all need and attachments to physical reality! In time this state brings pure consciousness.

There are many individuals who cannot meditate without the company of others or who must meditate with music. This may be acceptable in the first four stages as these stages belong to the realm of form and may be necessary for those who are beginners to the world of meditation. Until we are ready we should not expand our consciousness further through the higher realms.

Those who are ready to progress to the last stage the formless should realise the realm of form does not bring complete tranquillity, peace or control. When we want to expand consciousness we must learn to control the mind and go beyond, "I can't meditate without music! I can't meditate on my own!" Is hanging onto the objective world. To reach neutrality we must go beyond the needs and desires of objective existence, the world is ruled by our rational mind. Higher spiritual unfoldment must transcend objectivity and find the realm of subjectivity.

Therefore the last four stages of meditation help us to transform and transcend all objective existence to find a higher recognisance of pure consciousness. This is the pathway which brings clarity, insight, control and balance in a world of imbalance - the world of clutter, pain, obstacles and unfulfilment. In the higher scheme of things hanging onto the world of tangible reality and the desperate *need* for attachment, is not relevant to profound wisdom?

"You make the world with your own thoughts."

To reach this expanded consciousness we must first be able to distinguish between illusion and reality, true and false, right and wrong. Secondly we must have the power to discipline our mental faculties. Discipline means to discipline one's thoughts - to bring the mind under control. It stands to reason if we allow the mind to own us we are not in control. This then, is lack of mental empowerment which means our lives will lack peace, direction and harmony. Meditation gives us the ability to bring balance and peace back into our lives from the turmoil of exaggerated reality.

All the mind does is perceive the world of form of the objective world. Without the mind or thought there would be no objective existence. Our whole existence arises from our perceptions which is why we all see things differently. There are many thoughts some manifested through ignorance and others through the ignorance of our needs, desires and fantasies. When we penetrate the manifestations of our physical existence with clarity and wisdom, ignorance disappears and this world of objectivity becomes the delusion. Therefore to liberate the mind of all unnecessary clutter it is essential to free the mind through meditation. This will always help not only to purify our thought processes which gives us insight to grasp the conceptual reality of our existence but to also feed and nourish the spirit Neutrality can be eventually achieved through spiritual growth and the higher stages of meditation - the formless. There is no need to believe in a majestic God or any deity to reach this stage. That is the whole purpose - this is a stage of freedom. The ability to let go of the world of form - of illusion - even of one's own individuality. This is a state of pure consciousness and infinite wisdom.

"Become concerned with complexity and you will lose sight of simplicity."

Before we start to meditate we should learn to shut off from the many worries and cares of the world. Many years ago, I was one who would go to bed and let the mind become completely active. I could not sleep! I would allow the days activities to be reprogrammed and then allow my mind to be possessed by worries! What if's! If only's! Perhaps! and all sorts of negative energies. In other words - no trust or faith in anything. Then I found freedom! I read a book on how to control the mind.. It took me almost six months to teach myself this mind control discipline and to this day when I go to bed I can fall to sleep instantly.

The first step is to close your eyes and visualise a black sheet. Try not to let anything encroach on this blackness. This of course may be difficult

- but try all the same. After a while if you need a focus, visualise just one object. I used a tree. Just a simple tree - like one a child would draw. I would not allow the branches to sway or a bird to sit in my tree. I would focus on this every night until I had learnt to control the mind. I would not allow my thoughts to wander. Over active imagination can play havoc on our psyche so its reasonable to assume that we must discipline our mental faculties. Through this process I was eventually able to conquer my thoughts.

If there were things I was worried about I would say to myself," Tonight you will go out (astral travelling) and find the answers to your problems." This proved very successful as I always found solutions to many of the problems I encountered in the physical world. I was able to let go of worry and to have faith. To know and understand *'we have'* the answers and the Universe will always provide. Through these practices I was able to develop my intuitive abilities as well.

> **"All creatures are more than they seem.**
> **We are all more than we know."**

Through the mastery and conquest of the mental plane this then provides a clear link to the higher spiritual realms. Meditation becomes a means to provide that link to another dimension. Even if one prays it is essential to clear the mind through meditation or there can be no link to the other realms of consciousness.

Prayer or spiritual affirmations which seek purity in mind and spirit may be needed to nourish the soul and to inspire growth and higher consciousness. Positive reprogramming will always lead us to purer realms of spiritual understanding. It is pointless saying an affirmation just once as it must be said over and over again to get the message through. This is why I have kept repeating myself throughout this book!

"Repetition is the mother of skill."

The mind and the higher mind are the products of not just this lifetime but many lifetimes. Therefore we can assme there is a definite need to change and transform negative thoughts and perceptions to a more profound modality. It becomes the key not only to unlock but to *free* our imprisoned spirit.

Some weighed down by many lifetimes of suppressed emotions as well as those who have collected their own personal demons throughout this lifetime. There is also the insidious rubbish and clutter we take on board because we lose direction. Meditation becomes a means to bring more disciplined and purified thought processes into our everyday existence. Through the control and expansion of our mental faculties we can understand the spiritual significance of detachment.

Detachment does not mean we cannot love, share, care or understand. It just means we do not become limited and bound in earthly concerns. We do not become *imprisoned* with the insignificance of baser reality. Through the simple art of meditation we are able to achieve purification, control and peace of mind. When we learn this very valuable spiritual lesson we can then purify our whole system! Our lives will then take on completely new dimensions of awareness and perceptivity.

"Let me this day be positive and beautiful,
Let me this day be spiritual and loving,
Let me this day control my thoughts and imagination,
Let me this day shun all negativity.
Let me this day be Beauty, Light and Love;
Let me this day, direct my energies to everything which
has to be accomplished, so that my success is assured.
Today I am the master of my Destiny.
Today I control my Magnets of the Universe.

RE: *Magnets of the Universe*

I recommend the following technique for balancing the body and mind every day. This can be done anywhere, either sitting, standing or lying down.

Breath in through the nose and breath out through the mouth. On the in breath - breath in white or golden light and when breathing out - breath out rubbish - all the rubbish which has accumulated in the mind and body over the day. As one progresses it is surprising what can happen!

"A tranquil mind gives life to the soul."

This is not a chapter on meditation but on the essential use of meditation in our every day life. To learn meditation you may need to go to meditation classes. Some people cannot discipline the mind before they discipline the body and so they need some other form of metaphysical discipline to attain this. e.g. Yoga, Tai Chi or Chi Kung. Of course, even meditation demands that we relax the body first - every muscle and joint has to be relaxed thus achieving the best results from the meditative state.

Through the ability to meditate we will definitely learn to control some of the negativity ruling our every day life. It can help reverse the very structure of our day to day existence and instead of negative and undisciplined thoughts ruling us we can take charge and rule them.

It is very easy to lose direction in life! As a very dear friend aptly says," I've totally lost the plot!" Through the many responsibilities and commitments in life not only to ourselves but also to others it is very easy to miss the way. Our karmic growth and development demands we operate from four planes of existence. If we do not take time out for solitude and meditation how can we feed our soul?

It is impossible to journey on the path to expanded consciousness if we do not spend time with the inner self - the spirit. Through the ability to control the mind - we can then expand the mind - and direct all thoughts to higher dimensions of profound significance.

To do this we must *make time!* Nothing is impossible! If it was something tangible we would find the time easily enough! In the higher scheme of things seeking communion with our spirit is more precious than gold. We do not have to spend days in seclusion but it is essential that we spend time with the inner self. Eastern philosophers believe there are three stages to expanded consciousness or discipleship. The first is listening, the second is reflection and the third is meditation. These will in time promote the necessary catalyst for peace, insight, control and spiritual growth necessary on the journey to the light.

"Truth is as hard to find,
as buried water in a drought."

Many individuals spend their lives seeking perfection not only from themselves but from others. This can very often drive their families to distraction. They may be extremely loving and compassionate people but their need for perfection alienates the very ones they love the most. We must all realise we will never find complete perfection externally or internally and those who try, very often lose direction! Harmony, peace, tranquillity and positive insight can be found through meditation and is necessary for all who journey on this pathway in life. Why? Simply because we must first balance our own body and mind and spirit before we can see beyond misconceptions of the physical world. Meditation then is the mandatory means to unite our physical existence with the spiritual. The light of our spirit is the light we need to journey to expanded consciousness!

Pain can be alleviated through meditation. Controlling the mental process will create a positive responsiveness through the body. The mind is the centre of operations, it relays the messages to the rest of the body. Through thoughts and actions over many lifetimes we retain all sorts of negative rubbish which we then use to structure our lives.

Therefore time spent in solitude and meditation revitalises our spiritual senses and helps us penetrate the objective world of finite reality. In the future when constructing our homes it would definitely benefit everyone if a meditation room could be included in the building. This is vital to continue and maintain spiritual growth and balance in an ambiguous world of physical seduction. This would then become our private temple to create the environment needed to purify mind, body and spirit for the creation and recreation of our every day existence. Certainly *not* through ritual but through the ability to find peace and balance in a world full of imbalance. Through this modality we can then restructure and transform our lives from the past and present into positive accomplishments for the future. We can virtually set ourselves free from the imperfections of physical reality.

**"If a man's mind becomes pure,
so will his surroundings."**

Our mind is what envisages and creates so it has to be free and clear. Imagination has to flow but it does not have to rule. Imagination can be visionary but when out of control it can create disaster. Therefore to bring balance, harmony, peace and control, we must discipline ourselves through our thought processes. Meditation then connects our consciousness with the sublime and provides the nourishment necessary to expand and purify the enigmatic existence of physical reality.

My affirmation for expanding consciousness:

The Journey

"Let me not seek to manipulate others,
through my own egotism.
Let me not justify any wrong doing,
for my own gratification.
Let me not condone any falsehood,
because of my own lack of discernment.
Let me not fill my life, with my own
selfish needs and desires.
Let me not fail in my quest for truth, and guide
my footsteps towards expanded consciousness.
Let me find strength and love, in my own self-empowerment.
Let me uplift all those, who seek my council,
But not to give myself, in useless self-sacrifice.
Let me initiate, create and expand my work, for my
own Karmic and evolutionary growth and achievement.
Let me find joy, in purity of mind and spirit,
on my journey to freedom.
Let me complete the divine plan for my life,
through truth, faith, light and love."

CHAPTER 11

NEUTRALITY..... *"In all our many lifetimes, consciousness*

will evolve, towards knowing truth.

Nothing is lost and the whole becomes complete.

If there is a plan - it is for expanding

consciousness - to enlightenment."

Neutrality - the balancing of it all. The letting go of all limitation and bondage to the world of form. To know the world of form is created from the mind and to understand - the mind can set us free!

"A pure mind creates 'absolute' joy."

The higher we evolve the more letting go we have to accomplish. Our comprehension and perception changes the more we grow. The more we grow the more we penetrate the world of illusion which eventually inaugurates a deeper understanding into the higher realms of profound truths. This is why there are so many stages of transition in our lives. Very often people leave our lives, one way or another and we are faced with completely new circumstances which are contradictory to what we have previously seen as elementary to our physical existence. Eventually through this process we are able to comprehend the *need* for attachment is really an illusion.

As our higher consciousness expands we soon discover how difficult it is to live with the same conditions which we have previously tolerated. It is through this process we all experience an emotional death and rebirth. The more we evolve the more it becomes obvious we must create our own reality through higher mystical concepts. This progression will eventually bring us to the elevated state of expanded consciousness, detachment and neutrality.

> *"Where do we come from. Where do we go?*
> *Only the Wise man knows.*
> *Every day man learns something,*
> *Every day the Wise Man gives up something."*

Negativity arises from unruly thoughts, ignorance and perception. Our perception comes from our stages of awareness - from how we perceive life. Through the ability to understand truth and wisdom, ignorance disappears, perceptions change and the objective world becomes neutral.

As I have said before there are many degrees of ignorance. Some are born from pure ignorance and some from the ignorance of baser energies - of personal needs and desires. Self-awareness is only the beginning of our journey to the light of expanded consciousness.

Living life is like catching a lift. We all have choices! To go down to the basement, to the lower levels or to journey to the top floor. Sometimes we may get out to investigate the floors in between. This can very often prolong our journey with unnecessary clutter and baggage! Our progress is determined by our needs and desires and our need for evolutionary growth. The choice is up to us! We are responsible for our own journey - our own pathway. This is Karma - this is free will!

When we choose our lives - we choose from the outside looking in (from the Spirit World). When we are reborn to the earth plane we are on the inside looking in. What we must eventually achieve is to direct the consciousness to the outside - (the greater reality) to looking in. Then we see the physical world for what it is - a physical and transient dimension for evolutionary growth to the higher realms of spiritual understanding. This recognisance paves the way to neutrality and ultimately to freedom, the *freedom of our conscious mind*! This brings neutrality and ultimately liberation from the subjugation of all earthly concerns.

Try it and see. Pretend you are 'up there,' looking in. If you have already progressed to a cosmic awareness and understanding you will see everything 'down here' is only temporary and doesn't really matter in the higher scheme of things. Nonetheless because we all live in the physical realm we will still have to experience and understand physical reality to transcend it. Remember the whole purpose for earthly existence is immortality of the spirit. The cessation of life, death and rebirth to earthly encumbrances through divine love, faith and wisdom.

Liberation is not possible until we transcend emotional *needs and desires.* Growth must encompass all levels of existence; physically, emotionally, mentally and spiritually. I certainly do not mean we have to deny ourselves *love.* This is certainly not necessary for any attainment of neutrality or liberation.

We must expand the heart chakra to encompass a love which excludes need and all the limitations and bondage which emanate from this negative energy. Too many individuals use their heart chakra on a baser level. It is only when we transcend the love which limits and binds, are we able to expand the heart chakra in all of it's glory and power to become a beautiful celestial mass of energy. Therefore when we can substantially reduce the needs, desires and deceptions of physical reality we will understand the freedom which comes from detachment

Chakra means wheel or revolving disk. The Chakras are not situated in the human body but on the surface of the etheric double about seven millimetres above the surface of the skin. There are four grades of etheric matter. 1 st. - Etheric -This is the medium of ordinary current electricity and sound. 2nd. - Super Etheric - This is the medium of light. 3 rd. - Sub Atomic - This is the medium of the finer forces of electricity. 4 th. - Atomic - This is the medium for the transmission of thought from brain to brain.

The etheric double is called the vital body or the vehicle of vitality (Prana - Chi) which carries and distributes the intricate vital energy to vitalise the physical body. The Etheric Aura or Health Aura projects several centimetres from the skin of the body. Into the composition of the etheric double must enter something of all the different grades of etheric matter. The portions are determined by the race - the sub race and type of man or woman as well as the individual Karma.

There are seven atoms of Vitality Globules and these globules are dependent on light for their manifestation and are identified by the seven colour rays; red, orange, yellow, green, blue, indigo and violet. These globules can be seen in the atmosphere on a hot sunny day darting all around us. This vitality is absorbed by the etheric and physical bodies. The chakras are sources of light depressions of rapidly rotating matter. As these forces of vitality flow through the Chakras they vitalise the etheric double.

These forces are essential to the life of the etheric and to the physical body. This force varies with the individual degrees of evolutionary development. The higher one evolves the greater the vitality. When the individual has not progressed they glow duller and the etheric particles move lethargically just forming the vortex necessary for the transmission of the force and no more.

In those individuals who have progressed through evolutionary growth, the chakras glow and pulsate with a bright and blazing brilliance. These whirling masses of energy can be from five centimetres to fifteen centimetres in size depending on the development of the individual. In babies the centres are seven millimetres in size.

You can liken the spine to a stem of a flower and the chakras are the pulsating flower heads perpetually rotating and into the centre of these whirling masses a force or energy from the higher dimensions is always flowing. Without this energy the human body would be non-existent, therefore the centres are in operation in everyone sluggish or vital, depending on the evolutionary growth of the individual.

The Etheric chakras have two distinct functions - firstly to absorb and distribute vitality to the etheric body and then to the physical body - thus keeping these alive. Secondly to bring down into the physical consciousness whatever may be the quality in relationship to the comparable astral centre. Our astral or higher body has chakras in finer materials which correspond to the etheric chakras. The force or vitality we need comes from the astral plane, into the etheric. The chakras correspond to certain physical organs nearest to them - but we must be aware the chakras are not placed in the interior of the physical body but on the surface of the etheric double.

The top chakra is not theoretically classed as a chakra. The mystics call this the thousand petal lotus. This is a beautiful whirlpool of twelve undulations. When a person has progressed to an extremely high level of spiritual advancement this centre increases in size until it almost covers the top of the head.

At a *very advanced* level of attainment the chakra reverses itself and instead of being a depression in the etheric body like the other chakras - and a channel of reception, it becomes a centre of radiation standing out from the head like a dome, halo or fountain - literally a crowning of glory. This is the opening of the Kundalini power - a supreme spiritual power. This is illumination! When *fully* awakened the centre portion is a brilliant and gleaming white flushed with gold at it's heart.

It is not possible to balance chakras or to energise them except through our own vitality. In fact it can do more harm than good when we allow others to interfere with these energy disks. It is only through our own evolutionary growth and development we create vibrant, pulsating masses of energy. Through the ability to transcend and 'to overcome to become.' There is no quick solution to expanded consciousness. It only comes when we have transformed and transcended the residue from our past and present lives. It is essential for higher evolutionary growth and development to believe in ourselves unconditionally. *This is our vitality - our life force.* Then it is up to us to use this vital energy the right way - through positive attainments!

The Kundalini Power lies within us all. Until we awaken this power it lies coiled at the base of the spine like a serpent asleep. Once we become aware this power is aroused. It begins to uncoil itself and starts to enter the psychic nerve centres - our chakras - for awakening. Through our Karmic and evolutionary growth we are normally in control of these awakenings. Eventually through the higher realms of illuminated consciousness the serpent power reaches the thousand petal lotus in the brain-centre. This is the awakening of the full Kundalini power - a supreme spiritual power of knowledge and divine revelation. (Not channelled information from the world of spirit)

The awakening of full Kundalini power is not an easy energy to control. Those who have reached this stage have gone through years of denial and for many - pain as well, not just to open up this majestic energy but to learn to use it the right way through purified thoughts and actions. There is certainly no room here for negative perceptions. This is a journey of purified thoughts and deeds or they would not have lived to tell the tale. This is why it is called the serpent fire!

"Colour creates, it energises, it harmonises,
it warms, it cools, it feels, it expands,
it envisages, it diffuses, and it beautifies.
Colour is the pearl of wisdom, the essence of light,
the rainbow of life and the kaleidoscope,
of all creation."

Our chakras are the proof of who we are! Through the ability to transcend all negativity we are able to create dynamic, pulsating wheels of energy. If this then becomes our reality this poses another question, 'Why do we need to hang onto a divine deity for our spiritual power?'

> *"The world is a bridge,*
> *walk across,*
> *but build no house upon it."*

Our lives are ruled by Karma but through the requirement to change our perception in life and ourselves we can change our attitudes and patterning and therefore our Karmic returns. Neutrality does not mean complete denial. It means we have to transform and transcend the baser physical urges. To have - to need - to want.

It does not mean we cannot visualise, create and achieve through strength, discernment, integrity, morality and divine compassion. As we expand our consciousness to these higher levels our personal wants and needs fade anyway. They become secondary to humanitarian and spiritual reality. This strengthens the ability to ultimately penetrate all illusion. Neutrality then is just the balancing of it all!

> *"To see the truth, is not enough,*
> *But to 'use' truth, with purity of mind and spirit,*
> *this will bring freedom."*

Again we do not have to deny ourselves completely. As long as we know what is illusion and what is reality? Immortality of the spirit cannot come from focusing on earthly love, wealth, power and acquisitions but from our ability to overcome all superficial needs of our earthly desires. Our evolutionary and spiritual growth demands we journey towards the light of expanded consciousness and freedom - if not in this lifetime - then in our future incarnations.

Neutrality is letting go.

We still need to live within the confines of a physical existence. Our every day life entails many responsibilities not only for ourselves but for others. The means not to just provide food and clothing but all household expenses. Education and sickness benefits must be found and then there are humanitarian obligations which should be recognised throughout our lives. We still have to live in the physical world and pretending it doesn't exist is stupidity. This is why we are here in the first place. In a physical existence - with physical reality - to learn, to grow, to create and to evolve to expanded realms of discriminating wisdom.

Many monks give up everything and live in caves to find elightenment. This is not wrong - as many individuals choose a monastic life for the discipline needed to gain these mystical attainments. These are a minority and not completely necessary for illumination. We all need a certain amount of discipline and solitude to create any spiritual growth. There are those who co-exist in the physical world and have reached these exalted states without becoming monks. These states of attainment still demand solitude and a great deal of discipline, discrimination and denial in the physical realities of our western society. So the physical is here and so are we! However we need to know this is all it is. It is not immortality of the spirit! We do not have to worship or possess the entrapments of a physical existence. *Use* them by all means but do not hang onto them or need them to find freedom, peace or the joy of living.

What is loss? Loss of any kind be it physical, emotional or even spiritual is letting go, or reaching an end. For some, loss means absence, failure and deprivation. When we hang onto and become so attached to the many needs and fantasies of earthly desires we immerse ourselves in fear, heartache and even guilt from the many losses in our lives. When we transcend loss we transcend heartache and fear. This is the balancing of it all! This is neutrality - liberation from all...

Physical manifestations and earthly encumbrances.

To know and understand the who and what we are and our true purpose is to comprehend the meaning of life. Many religious cults go to extremes. Too expansive or too much suppression. These extreme measures are not necessary for higher spiritual unfoldment and liberation and in many instances will have to be corrected in some future lifetime. The middle way is the journey to the light of expanded consciousness and freedom. Obsessive denial and suppression very often come from humility, guilt and fear. Over expansiveness from lack of discipline and boundaries.

Enlightenment and illumination are definitely higher spiritual attainments that do necessitate a certain amount of denial with discipline and discrimination simply because one is being purified for more esoteric knowledge and crystallisation. Conviction from the deepest seat of consciousness develops into spiritual surety. This in turn creates an infallible knowing in which the knower is unmistakably one with divine knowledge.

"Sometimes to fight evil is to strengthen it,
so the sage merely pass it by."

It is only through the ability to transcend the negative emotions and attitudes which imprison us to the physical world in the first place we can eventually find neutrality. The next stage is one of freedom and liberation and this means no more bonding or cording to the earth plane - but to transcend and go beyond.

The necessity to change our perceptions of life comes through knowledge, truth and evolutionary growth. The mind must be clear and free from interference for a direct link to the higher realms of perceptivity. Adults as well as children must have certain guide lines to live productive and positive lives. This is essential for Karmic and evolutionary growth and to attain to a higher level of self-awareness. This then gives us the ability to elevate our minds and hearts to achieve *God Consciousness.*

"An intelligent mind acquires knowledge,
but the ear of the wise, seeks knowledge."

When individuals are ready for neutrality or the exalted states of illumination and enlightenment one can actually break these boundaries of the physical, emotional, mental and spiritual worlds and go beyond.

There is then no fear of misusing and abusing the knowledge and power which comes from these lofty realms. Through purified thoughts and deeds they have expanded their psyche to greater receptivity to encompass the sublime.

We can find liberation from the earth plane when we have transcended all the dross of past lives no matter what religion we believe in. This realm deals with form! On the other hand illumination and enlightenment can only be experienced when we transcend all thoughts of majestic beings or Gods. This realm deals with the formless. Neutrality is when we go beyond the boundaries of our own ego or through the interaction of a supreme deity, such as God.

This world of neutrality is often misunderstood and many believe it is a void of the intellect and in a sense this is so. Nevertheless neutrality is *not* a world of nothing! It is a state of all encompassing freedom, it is beauty, it is light, it is celestial love, it is non-attachment, it is seeing, it is knowing, it is infinite, it is serenity, it is wisdom, it is pure consciousness and a state of *'the divine mind.'*

Not everyone is ready for meditation but when they are meditation opens the line to our higher consciousness. The link it creates should be free from the intrusions of the physical dimension. To find neutrality, we even transcend individualisation. This is not a contradiction. For positive evolutionary growth we *must* learn to believe in ourselves, we must individualise. Neutrality then is the next step to freedom. We must believe in self - to transcend self. We must understand the illusion of life - to understand the illusion of death. Then we must transcend life - to transcend death.

"The eye of knowledge sees with the most clarity."
Truth is the greatest atonement.
Attachment is the worst of all sorrows.
Detachment is the source of lasting happiness."

"The Way of Kings.
Ancient Wisdom from the Sanskrit Vedas.
(Translated by Drew Lawrence)

CHAPTER 12

LIBERATION...... *"Like a mountain, a good man*

is visible from afar. What is

goodness? You already know.

If goodness is like a mountain,

it is hard to achieve the summit.

The 'master' goes beyond the

boundless land and nothing,

neither, man, demon or gods,

nothing in all creation can

hold him."

Many will reach liberation and/or illumination this lifetime, others will come back and hopefully next lifetime find their freedom. Many, many, many others will have quite a few lifetimes before they reach the light of infinite wisdom. Why? Simply because of the negative choices these individuals make in their lives. Whatever we choose not to do we have to come back and redo. Whatever we do the wrong way and do not consciously change in this life we will have to eventually put it right in future incarnations. We are all born with special talents, skills and attributes. Through negativity emotional needs and ignorance we very often fail our Karmic and evolutionary responsibilities by not developing and using these divine gifts. Cultivating all positive energies revitalises and transports one's psyche on a wave of indefinite power. It is only when we start to question do we start our journey of self-awareness and then we have the ability to tap into a supreme spiritual power to find the light of *absolute wisdom.*

"Who shall conquer the world? Who shall conquer death? Who shall discover the shining way? You shall!"

If the mind has not reached it's potential, is lazy or closed, it stands to reason it needs to be awakened. As I have said before we are one tenth conscious and nine tenths subconscious. Even though we may not want to admit it, many of us do not even develop our minds and higher minds to half this potential. If we did - why have we been so long on the journey to freedom and liberation? The mind cannot be awakened just through rational means. The purely rational world is all a world where we recognise only baser realities.

We must include the world of the irrational - the world we cannot see. Of course there are those who seek just the rational and there are those who are nothing but irrational. The middle way is the only way - the golden way!

To awaken the intellect one needs - to use it, to exercise it, to educate it, to control it and to own it. Education, study and reading are needed to awaken the intellect. The ability to elevate our thought processes allows us to see things through a much broader expansive but rational perspective. In other words we expand the mind through intelligent means. The pathway to neutrality and wisdom is through the control of our mental energies!

Why is it so important to conquer and develop our mental faculties to find the higher realms of spirituality? Simply because we cannot discriminate or investigate with validation that realm which encompasses the more esoteric planes of awareness. This can very often create closed and even rigid perceptions and understanding not only ourselves but our spiritual philosophies. Self-awareness then becomes the key to unlock the mysteries of who we are, where we are going and why we are here!

In this day of new age concepts there are those who are embracing "Pixi Dust" philosophies. They believe profound spirituality and liberation does not require strength, discipline, responsibility or *discrimination*. Karma is of course choice! The choices between right or wrong! Illusion and reality! Light and darkness! Karma will lead us all to the point of no return eventually through unfulfilment, desolation and even sickness. Then we will definitely have to start questioning the meaning of life and ourselves. It creates the ability to bring a greater comprehension of infinite truth and wisdom through the conscious mind. This then creates the ability to cross those barriers to the light of acute contemplation and insight.

> ***"Happy is the man who finds wisdom!***
> ***and the man who gets understanding,***
> ***for the gain from it is better than***
> ***gain from silver and its profit better than gold."***

4,000 years ago, The Age Of Aries began and this brought humanity to the crossroads. The key phrase of Aries, "I Am." Eventually humanity started to question the who and what they were. "The I Am!" The early philosophers were trying to create a new kind of rationalisation and started questioning the traditional myths. They started to look at the irrational world and created another dimension to transcend the confines of agrarian mysticism and civic veneration - their world of many Gods! They had started to investigate the supernatural and gladly surrendered to this new profound religious thinking.

The world of many Gods brought much chaos, delusion and fantasy, so things had to change. The evolutionary growth of humanity at this stage had not progressed very far - certainly not as far as it has today. The karmic and evolutionary wheel had turned. A new teacher and messenger by the name of Moses, one of the many appearing down through the ages, was born to Earth. Again the truth was distorted through egotism and power but it brought organised spiritual and evolutionary growth out of disorganised baser and chaotic belief systems. A messenger and teacher was also chosen to enlighten the peoples of the East. Once again truth became misunderstood and the religion became very extreme but true spiritual faith - without a need for a Divine Deity - blossomed.

Eventually - The Age Of Pisces brought a new leader and teacher. This became an extremely deceptive age and the truth was again omitted enabling men to control society through greed and manipulative power. Through the years the one God principle spread throughout most of the world. Because of this gross misinterpretation it failed to teach humanity faith in self but it did teach faith. The faith which transcended the rational. Because of the distortion and misconception of the truth, humanity still needed a Divine deity - a God - for spiritual faith as they still had not yet learnt to empower themselves spiritually. The Age of Pisces unfolded with many deceptions (Neptune qualities) but humanity found faith - the faith in the irrational - the unseen.

Who is God? Why did people believe in many Gods in the past? They did so because this was the extent of evolutionary growth at the time. These beliefs were created from the stories and fables brought about through the earthly visits of the chariots of the Gods. The navigators of these chariots were 'The Gardeners Of The Earth.' Through the deception which followed these Gardeners eventually had to leave. What developed through the many centuries which followed - as all good legends do - were stories and great myths about the wonders of these great 'Gods.' How easy that would be when one considers some of the information and misinformation which is being created at this point in time! It seems we are still repeating negative patterning just as we have done in the past!

One of the meanings for '*God*,' is authority and power. This is what the word God means, *those with higher authority* referring to - The Gardeners of the Earth. Take a look at ancient mythology. These are the stories and fables about the wonders of these heavenly beings and how the mortal world could overcome the many obstacles of life through courage, faith, imagination and self-empowerment. However no matter how brave these mortals were physically, emotionally and mentally they were still unable to believe in their own spiritual power. Through the manipulation of the priests they still needed to have someone else to believe in - a Divine Deity!

Greed and idolatry very often corrupts those who seek power! Therefore the truth was omitted and those in higher positions began to manipulate and control the masses. As a consequnce what would have happened if humanity had become empowered and believed in themselves unconditionally - physically, emotionally, mentally *and* spiritually? They wouldn't have needed to be controlled by priests in the first place! So those with assumed spiritual authority became extremely egotistical and wanted the position and power of not only the great Pharaohs and Emperors who were worshipped like God-Kings but also of the legendary, celestial "Gardeners Of The Earth."

Therefore they had to become the representative of not just any God but *'The God.'* This would create the power they needed to control the masses! This is why the Karmic and evolutionary wheel must keep turning until we penetrate this world of illusion. Where we can have faith - not in a divine being - but faith in our own being - and then to use this power for the *good* of all humanity.

Remember the very funny movie, 'The God's Must Be Crazy?' This film is about a bottle, thrown from a plane. The natives thought it fell out of the sky and therefore presumed it must have come from heaven! They could not comprehend this bottle could have come from anything or anyone but from the 'Gods' themselves as their understanding and information of the outside world was non-existent. Perception therefore is not only based on the assimilation and comprehension of knowledge but also on the availability of knowledge and of course, truth.

Our knowledge of God comes to us from the Bible. The Bible was edited by the selfish and manipulative priests who needed to control through their own power. Even now, new knowledge has surfaced about sections which have been removed plus the fact when this book was written, it was written by the priests themselves, from the legends and information which had come down through time. Think about a movie script, does the movie ever follow the book precisely or do they change the script to suit those making the movie?

Belief in God creates our need to depend on a Divine Deity for happiness and direction. We fail to empower ourselves for our own spiritual growth. We are certainly not alone just because we do not believe in God! It just means we can go beyond the confines of a majestic entity for faith and guidance. Faith then has no barriers! True self-empowerment creates the ability to create faith in self. There are no reasons to blame God or anyone else for our misfortunes or to bless God for our happiness. We become personally responsible for everything we are and everything we do! This is Karma!

God does not pick our lives for us, we do - with a little help sometimes from the 'heavenly council.' The laws of the Universe are love, integrity, morality, truth and faith. The golden rules - *To thine own self be true* and *Do unto others as you would have them do unto you.'* Through the ability to live our lives by these philosophies we cancel all negativity and the need for protection especially the protection of a Divine Deity.

If you cannot yet grasp these truths they will soon be given through a new divine teacher and his assistants. There will be those who still choose not to believe until they themselves penetrate illusion through their own evolutionary growth and development. That is choice and we are all responsible for our own choices! This is Karma - this is justice!

Thankfully there will be many who will *know* simply because they are ready! The age of Aquarius will bring Truth, Knowledge and divine compassion for all humanity.

"Some people are born knowing,
some learn through open minds and hearts,
others stumble and fall then discover.
Heartache and loss, give many the need to seek and find.
Still others swim around in a sea of fear
and despair, clutching at life, needing something
to bring them peace and fulfilment.
Which one are you?
It does not matter! As long as you eventually
penetrate the world of illusion and find your
freedom. Then you to can fly like the eagle,
in the ultimate realisation of spiritual
consciousness."

RE *Magnets of the Universe*

Letting go of dogma and rigid perceptions is evolutionary and Karmic growth. Many individuals are consumed by fear and guilt because of these belief systems. A friend recently confided to me about the molestation she and her sister had endured from several men, (supposedly friends of the family) when they were little girls. Nothing was ever done because of biased, religious belief systems and of course fear. Her father even commented, it must have been their fault and at the time the girls believed him. (Not any more - thankfully) His rigid beliefs dictated that men were *not* responsible for their own actions.

There was no accountability for their own perverted actions. Women and even children were responsible for the sexual perversion of men! It appears sex is the sin of women! These are the biased, unjust and selfish concepts from the Bible! This is what many have been allowed to believe from the past and to this present day! This is religious dogma, suppression and reprisal! This is not *love* - spiritual or otherwise and it is certainly not positive self-empowerment, physically, emotionally, mentally *or* spiritually!

Proverbs: 17:16

"Why should a fool have a price in his hand to buy wisdom, when he has no mind."

Each and every one of us is responsible for our actions! We will all reap what we have sown in the past, present and in the future. This is Karma and Karma is the link in the perpetual chain of life, death and rebirth for our evolutionary growth. This is why we should never harbour judgment, hate, bitterness or revenge. These energies will always bind us to the limitation and bondage of earthly illusion. Karma gives us the means to transcend selfish and manipulative needs and desires to a more advanced sanctuary of divine love and wisdom. How? Simply through the ability to try again, again and yet again. To overcome we will always become!

There are many individuals who cannot comprehend the reasons why we must let go of resentment, bitterness and even guilt. Particularly when we are violated and sabotaged through the negative actions of others. To let go of these feelings we have to be aware the perpetrators which in many instances includes parents, come from pure ignorance or from the ignorance and selfishness of their baser needs and desires. Remember, *'Ignorance is the root of all evil.'*

However when we have to experience these traumatic circumstances it is very often because we ourselves have misused our sexuality in previous lifetimes. Whatever the reason we will still have to learn to let go of all negative emotions eventually to set ourselves free. We certainly do not have to love or even learn to love those who have mistreated us. Nevertheless we do have to transcend hate, bitterness, resentment and guilt if we do not want to come back with extreme negativity or with these same individuals in future lifetimes By becoming completely indifferent to these people and their negative action we can eventually journey to the exalted states of neutrality. This is freedom! Our destination to the higher realms of consciousness can only be accomplished through acceptance and through the purification of all thoughts and deeds. When we experience extreme love or hate we will be Karmicly bonded in future lifetimes. Therefore when we finally reach neutrality we transcend imprisonment to the baser reality of all earthly fallibility. To *transcend reasoning we transcend all objective existence!* This is indeed freedom!

"From a quiet mind comes vision;
From vision comes knowledge of unity;
From unity comes compassion for all;
From compassion comes greatness."

In the higher scheme of things *the divine* are only interested in our evolutionary and Karmic growth to the expanded realms of purified thoughts and deeds.

Humanity is on the threshold of a new age and this means we are all going to experience cataclysmic changes not only for ourselves but for the world. This is needed to generate positive growth and development for all humanity into the next 2,000 years. This will bring to humanity greater expansion than ever before in the history of the world! Truth and the ability to use it changes, creates, beautifies, regenerates, frees and empowers on all planes of existence.

This new age brings a new divine teacher and leader who will have the tremendous task of imparting truth, knowledge and the ability to love with divine compassion all humanity, to a world which lacks discernment, responsibility and morality. This will eventually bring to the surviving humanity a higher realisation of spiritual truths and understanding.

"There is gold and abundance of costly stones,
but the lips of knowledge are a precious jewel."

The Aquarian Age will establish humanitarian and spiritual values essential for the evolution of humankind. This will be an age of truth and knowledge. Eastern mysticism has filtered through to provide whole new dimensions for expanding consciousness. Humankind will learn to believe in self - to empower self! To learn indeed faith can move mountains - that is faith in self. Not to lean on the power of a majestic

God being - but to learn to come from one's own power. The energy which comes from an individuals etheric double is tremendous - this is our vitality (Prana - Chi) our life force. Most of us completely deny the power and energy which we have within us - and look to find it within something or someone else.

We virtually prostitute ourselves! We want a crutch - we need support, we need a divine entity - a divine God. Why is it so hard to understand that we can through our own power of truth, divine love and faith, transcend all negativity! The ability to transform all our negative energies into favourable ones through positive self-empowerment, physically, emotionally, mentally *and* spiritually.

This will mean we do not have to rely on a majestic power such as God - to create the miracles in our lives. This power belongs to each and every one of us! Through this energy we can create our own miracles as this is what our own divine power gives us. The evolutionary and karmic wheel keeps turning and we keep turning with it until we transcend the deceptions of physical reality.

"Do not speak in the hearing of a fool,
for he will despise the wisdom of your words."

Buddhist's believe everyone has the ability to attain to Buddhahood. Basically this means everyone can become illuminated or enlightened through the ability to journey on the right path with the right aspirations. This journey to the light does not include a belief in a divine 'One God' principle.

God consciousness means the same. God is *not* a being! God is *not* an energy! *God is a consciousness!* A consciousness of purity, truth and love. The consciousness we must all strive for and attain! Any state of *being,* is a consciousness! Belief in God creates faith. Belief in anything creates faith! This does not mean there is a God! Faith is the energy! This is why faith creates miracles. Faith is majestic power! Faith can move mountains - faith in anything - especially the self.

"Truth will always set us free."

Numerologically *'God'* vibrates to 17/8. This means immortality, revelation, truth and wisdom mastered through strength, discipline, discrimination, self-empowerment, courage, responsibility and Karma. It is universal healing, truth and understanding. 8 is authority. It is material and spiritual freedom. The soul of God is 6 = Balance gained through love and responsibility.

Therefore *God consciousness* is the ability to strive for the immortality of our spirit through purified thoughts, deeds and faith. To end our rounds of existence on the earth plane by using discipline, discrimination, truth and love to become empowered on all planes of existence.

We must be aware that we are not automatically *God Consciousness.* If we were we wouldn't be here! There are a few lucky souls who will find liberation this lifetime and those who have reached enlightenment and illumination through the opening of the thousand petal lotus of the Kundalini power. Always a last life!!

God consciousness is the state we must all strive for and attain on our journey to the light of esoteric wisdom. What are the means to achieve these exalted states? Simply our Karmic and evolutionary growth. To overcome we will all become! We do not have to be perfect but we do have to cross those barriers to the light of celestial awareness to find neutrality and liberation.

This is the final chapter to our continual rounds of death and rebirth to physical existence. Then we go onto another dimension, a dimension which transcends all the limitations and bondage which is present on this, the plane of physical ambiguity.

Liberation - this is mastery! This is victory! This is the pot of gold at the end of the rainbow! The end of being corded to all physical attachments. We must always try to use the power of the mind to create - but we must also open the doors of the mind to expand to the higher realms of truth and understanding. Liberation from the earth plane does not necessarily mean the achievement of illumination and enlightenment - but these exalted states can be accomplished with a little more personal effort.

"The purpose in a man's mind is like deep water but a man of understanding will draw it out."

Very often our thought processes, our belief systems and our perceptions must change to bring about higher growth and spirituality. Too frequently we reject the changing of ideas and ideals because they are the very things which bring with them comfort and support. For many it also creates the path of least resistance. To change means we have to *let go*! and *letting go* brings fear, disorientation and panic. For many letting go is a gradual process and it may take several lifetimes.

This is why humanity has so much heartache! There are those who do not know how to change and those who do not want to change. Eventually when we can and do transform our thoughts, vision and perceptions we are able to transcend all earthly encumbrances. This then gives us the motivation and inclination to journey towards the light and to finally find the greatest prize of all - neutrality and liberation. This is our final Karmic reward!

> *"Faith creates, it manifests, it visualises,*
> *it projects, it invents, it conceives, it constructs,*
> *it produces, it establishes, it fabricates, it forms,*
> *it composes, it originates and it generates."*

The negative manifestations of all physical existence are the energies which confine us to the earth plane. Our goals in life should not be through the greed, need and desire of baser reality but through the ability to expand consciousness for liberation. This gives us the ability to journey to freedom through happiness, love, faith and divine power.

If our needs and desires involve the reality of another be careful - it may not be included in the *divine plan* for your life. This could be interfering in the reality of another human being. Manipulation through these needs and desires can definitely slow down our evolutionary growth and development and create more negative patterning.

If we believe in angels we will see angels. This does not mean there are angels. The mind creates what it believes which can have disastrous effects over many lifetimes if our thoughts are not based on higher moral and ethical standards. Even our visions are created through the faith of our beliefs systems. If one believes in Buddhism it would not do any good if they had a vision of the Virgin Mary. Or vice versa.

Our beliefs systems therefore dictates our visions! This is the power of faith! Faith is majestic power! Imagine what we could all achieve if we gave that much faith to ourselves through positive means. Let go and set yourself free. Become empowered and cross the barrier to the light of higher knowledge and truth. Not through intellectualising spirituality but through infinite wisdom. A very dear friend felicitously calls those who intellectualise spirituality - 'space cadets!'

The heavenly organisation is only one of many dimensions in the sea of space. There are many other centres in existence than the ones we mere mortals can understand and accept. There are still many on the earth plane who cannot even comprehend heaven let alone anything else.

Remember Earth is only the kindergarten of knowledge. Thankfully consciousness evolves! Because we have not yet learnt to empower ourselves through truth, faith and pure love (without warfare) we are not yet worthy of becoming involved with those with greater authority.

The Gardeners of the Earth, as well as those from the Heavenly Fields throughout time have always created the opportunities for the designated 'Leaders and Teachers of Divine Knowledge' here on Earth.

Even now there are those special teachers and leaders who have been born to earth to impart knowledge for the new age. They know who they are because of the circumstances which surround their initiation and if you could understand and experience what their initiation involved you wouldn't want to be one!

> ***"You are the one who will profit if you have wisdom and if you reject it, you are the one who will suffer."***

Liberation from the earth plane has come to many regardless of belief systems. This comes to those who finally transform and regenerate themselves by living their lives through *God Consciousness*. The 'lost souls' as I have said before, are the ones who do not believe in life after death and therefore create in the after life, fog and darkness. They cannot enter the heavenly fields until they believe! Those who choose to hang onto the earth plane for whatever reason will experience the same fate.

We have now come to another crossroad in the evolution of humankind. This is the dawn of a new age - an age of higher truth and knowledge - an age where love and divine compassion will unite humanity. This age takes us out of the darkness and heads us towards golden light. This will be when all is said and done *The Golden Age*. A time for change, where old belief systems and structures fall to make way for the new. This will bring greater unfoldment, expansion and wisdom to all those who will accept these higher truths.

It doesn't matter what we think or what we believe in. If we have not transcended earthly illusion and live our lives through the light of purified thoughts and deeds we will have to come back yet again. We come back until we overcome all limitation and bondage to earthly needs and desires. The sooner we understand and accept truth the sooner we reach our destination. This is of course choice! Karma is choice! This is why we have been so long on the path because all too often we make the wrong choices! The laws of the universe are fixed! They do not change, we do! Even if it takes many lifetimes!

Consciousness must evolve!

"By wisdom a house is built and by understanding it is established."

Evil - look at this word. When we turn the word around it reads - *Live.* Therefore all evil is living life back to front. It is going backwards in life, not forward. It is going backwards - into darkness. It is only when we go forward do we travel towards the light. Going backwards means not only hanging onto the past but using negative energies in which to live our lives. In many instances it is also created from our inefficiency to perceive the meaning of life! A lot of heartache can be avoided by changing our negative perceptions. It is not 'what humanity can do for me but what *I can do* for humanity.' Through the ability to have faith, love and joy in eternal life comes a higher perspective on our everyday living. Negative energies will always plunge us into darkness whereas positive energies lead us to the light of esoteric knowledge.

"Wisdom is a fountain of life to him who has it,
but folly is the chastisement of fools."

This is certainly not a pathway for the weak or fainthearted. This is definitely a journey which requires not only strength, discrimination and love but responsibility, faith and joy. The journey of darkness encompasses so many more heartaches which are not included in the divine plan. This is the journey which takes us backwards, these are the energies of *evil*. These are the negative energies which limit and bind us to continual life, death and rebirth.

Liberation - the end of our life on the earth plane! To escape the confines of Karmic bonding for freedom. To reach the ultimate of *God consciousness*. Liberation then becomes the Karmic obligation for all of us whatever our belief systems, ideas, ideals - or reality.

In the higher scheme of things, (I do not mean the world of spirit but the heavenly council) they record the truth! When all is said and done this is only earth school - the school of hard knocks. A world of ignobility and mediocrity. All the heartaches, pain and unfulfilment from the many experiences of life will in time teach us to escape from the cycle of negative patterning created from the earth plane, physical, emotional, mental and spiritual bondage.

It is only when we are in the heavenly fields and in spirit form we can judge if we have 'overcome to become.' It will certainly not be through our conscious thought patterns. Heaven does not need to judge! Through Karma - *'We will all reap what we sow!'*

Do not spend your life condemning others or those who are not as you are. Do not judge others because they do not believe as you do. Always remember that consciousness evolves! There will always be those who are not ready to change and those who do not want to change.

Let them go; find your own path. You are responsible for your own life, your own growth, your own choices. This is Karma! This is justice!

Very soon humanity will experience a great crucifixion creating heartaches, chaos, loss and death of the highest magnitude. This is definitely necessary for a change in mass consciousness. Through the downfall we will create whole new realities on all levels of existence. Only through the positive energies of hope, optimism, love, faith, acceptance and truth will humanity create new structures, ideals and ideas for our new age, *The Golden Age.* Open the mind and be ever alert for the new Messiah and his disciples who will provide humanity with divine truth and knowledge to help motivate and guide us into the next 2000 years.

The Karmic and evolutionary wheel keeps turning and we keep turning with it. This then is our journey - the journey of many lifetimes - the journey we all have to travel. "Crossing the Barrier To The Light Of Expanded Consciousness." This is our freedom the immortality of our spirit from the constraints of an enigmatic and deceptive world. So whatever we have to learn we will learn no matter how long it takes! Reincarnation gives us the ability to transform, regenerate and to transcend - to overcome to become and to live our lives through truth, faith, beauty, light, love and an expanded consciousness.

"To-morrow, and to-morrow, and to-morrow
Creeps in this pretty pace from day to day,
to the last syllable of recorded time;
And all our yesterdays have lighted fools
the way to dusky death. Out, out brief candle!
Life's but a walking shadow; a poor player,
that struts and frets his hour upon the stage
Then is heard no more."

Shakespeare's - Macbeth.

THE AGE OF AQUARIUS & CAPRICORN

2 0 0 0 - 4 0 0 0

THE AGE OF AQUARIUS - (I KNOW)

2000 - 3000: The time for a new Leader/Teacher and his assistants to guide and motivate us into the next 2000 years. They will impart truth, knowledge and the need to unite humanity through divine compassion and love. This heralds a new beginning for all humankind and will bring many, many, changes for peace in the world. There will be group discussions for solving problems in many areas of contention. This has already started for there are many self-awareness and therapy groups which help individuals by bringing them together to solve the many complexities and difficulties of life.

The actual age of Aquarius begins 2026. This age is one of peace so before this age can begin we must create peace. Numerologically, 2026=10/1. This is a new beginning. The bridge between heaven and earth. The ability to bring peace to people or to bring people together in peace. 26 is the number of Karma!

There will be more emphasis on this ability to bind together and to also solve the many important social issues which involve families, communities, governments and all humanity. This is a time for group involvement! Peace will create a greater awareness for friendship, fellowship and love. This is a time for unity and tolerance! Women will regain balance and through their own empowerment hold many positions of leadership. Of course this will also bring positive change to the consciousness of men. This will enable humanity to see and create whole new dimensions for equality and the ability to structure humanitarian concepts for all. A time when humankind will know truth, knowledge and love is the only way we can create a more caring, sharing and peaceful world. A time for greater insight and psychic awareness! There will of course be peaceful co-existence with those from other worlds throughout the *Golden Age*.

Environmentally solar power will be used throughout the world for energy. Shopping centres will be under one huge structure encased in glass or it's equivalent. This will provide the basis necessary for maintaining solar power energy. Everything including roadsides will be extremely clean, neat and tidy. City centres will no longer exist because they create nucleus for mass congregation. Private homes will be surrounded by the 'balance of nature'. These predictions like all predictions are only probability simply because karma is choice, it is still up to humanity to create its ultimate destiny.

3000 - 4000: This is a time for greater creativity, humanitarianism and unity together through faith, optimism and love. There will be complete equality for all humanity because this is a time for total acceptance. This is an abundant time! A time for freedom and expansion. A time to expand inner creativity and then to give this out to others. Beauty, faith, happiness and love will create new structures, ideals, ideas and philosophies. There will be a zest for life and a joy in living! Architecture, art, music and all the creative arts and sciences will flourish. Humanity will use faith to empower self! There will no doubt be interplanetary visits as this is a time for great expansion. Psychic abilities will be developed by the majority.

Eventually towards the end of this age the negative will start to infiltrate and much of humanity will become complacent, indulgent, extravagant, frivolous and even deceitful. Many will procrastinate, become too expansive, lazy, promiscuous and scatter their energies. There will be those who deny positive achievement through work, discipline, order, responsibility and organisation. The laws of morality, decency and integrity will again be cast aside. Another Sodom and Gomorroh! Sounds familiar?

4000 - 5000

THE AGE OF CAPRICORN - (I USE)

4000 - 5000: This is a new beginning - a reconstruction for humanity. A new Teacher/Messenger and assistants will teach humanity it is not just knowing truth which creates wisdom but the ability to use it with strength, discipline, responsibility, discrimination and love. This is the only pathway for positive karmic and evolutionary growth and development! Humanity will need to work to bring law, order and system out of chaos! This will again create whole new structures for humankind, to empower self. To climb to the top of the mountain of attainment on all plains of existence. The need to create tangible reality will bring humanity out of self-indulgence to create a time of stability and practicality. This is a time for reconstruction for all, through positive organisation! To balance the rational world with the irrational! To understand we all have to achieve to create any growth and expansion into the higher realms of all spiritual conviction.

5000-5999: This is the time for change and the time for freedom! This is the crossroads mental discernment versus physical reality. A time when humanity will progress through the ability to use love, knowledge, truth and faith for it's ultimate realisation - wisdom! To use *the mind* with pragmatic reasoning and creative sensitivity will change consciousness to untold dimensions of reality. To learn, to digest, to educate, to know, to expand, to change and to adapt humankind will be able to bring all the knowledge and traits of the past into higher dimensions, physically, emotionally, mentally and spiritually. To penetrate the world of illusion through discrimination. Mental discernment versus physical reality! Truth versus illusion! Light versus darkness! Good versus evil.

The ability to regenerate the psyche by cleansing the body and mind through the control of the five senses. This is freedom! The mind is what limits and binds us to physical reality in the first place therefore the mind can set us free! To transcend the purely physical existence through discriminating wisdom. The ability to use *the power of the intellect* to expand to the higher realms of psychic awareness and spiritual enlightenment. Self-empowerment on all plains of existence - *This is wisdom!* "To cross the Barrier To The Light Of Expanded Consciousness." This is the journey to neutrality and freedom! This is liberation from the world of encapsulation and the perpetual cycle of life, death and rebirth. This is Victory!

'The jigsaw Puzzle of our lives,
so many pieces,
Scattered so far and wide.
Blindfolded we look for them,
Valiantly searching.
Sometimes we find one;
Then struggle to make it fit.
Often we cannot find it's place,
Then impatiently throw it aside.
Later realising where it goes,
We pick it up again
and place the
missing piece.'

John K Reichstein